Twayne's United States Authors Series

Sylvia E. Bowman, *Editor*

INDIANA UNIVERSITY

Barrett Wendell

TUSAS 261

Barrett Wendell

Barrett Wendell

By ROBERT T. SELF

Northern Illinois University

TWAYNE PUBLISHERS

A DIVISION OF G. K. HALL & CO., BOSTON

Library of Congress Cataloging in Publication Data

Self, Robert T.
  Barrett Wendell.

  (Twayne's United States authors series)
  Bibliography: pp. 169–76.
  Includes index.
  1. Wendell, Barrett, 1855–1921.
PS3158.W7Z73   818'.4'09   75-12735
ISBN 0-8057-7160-3

For my Father and Mother

Contents

About the Author

Robert T. Self received his Masters degree from the University of Chicago and his Ph.D. from the University of North Carolina. Since 1969 he has been an assistant professor at Northern Illinois University where he teaches film, fiction, and American literature. He has published "The Correspondence of Amy Lowell and Barrett Wendell, 1915–1919" in the *New England Quarterly*. From this study of Wendell, he has prepared a critical edition of Wendell's writing, *The Selected Essays of Barrett Wendell* to be published by the John Colet Press Archive of American Literature, 1620–1920.

Preface

George Santayana's term the "Genteel Tradition" has become a pejorative catch-phrase to dismiss the efforts of many late nineteenth-century writers like Barrett Wendell (1855–1921). Any attempt objectively to analyze Wendell and his era must get beyond the negative attitudes of literary historians in the 1920s and 1930s which have obscured the significance of Wendell's teaching and writing. Despite the fact that Wendell saw himself as a weak successor to the Boston Brahmins, and despite the pressure of his aristocratic heritage, his famous conservative prejudice, and his physical weakness—which left him a character caught between the world of the old New England renaissance and the world of new literary creativity in the twentieth century—Wendell's role in American literary history was an important one.

As a teacher at Harvard from 1880 to 1917, he stood out as an eccentric rebel, for he refused to accept Charles Eliot's educational reforms in one of Harvard's golden eras; he was one of the major forces behind the concept of general education in the first decade of this century; and his courses in English composition and creative writing attracted students from all over the country and pioneered the techniques employed in such courses today. In 1897 he taught one of the first courses in American literature; and his concern "to think things together" led, in Harvard's honors degree in history and literature, to one of the first American studies programs. Moreover, his influence on young writers and critics like George Santayana, Amy Lowell, Robert Herrick, Edwin Arlington Robinson, George Pierce Baker, John Manly, Karl Young, Van Wyck Brooks, V. L. Parrington, and Horace Kallen was real and direct. Wendell fostered an atmosphere of encouragement to the creative artist at turn-of-the-century Harvard. Many of the students who passed through Wendell's classes became leaders in the literary revolution that Wendell himself foresaw but lacked the courage to lead.

As a literary historian, Wendell's significance is no less marked. His *Cotton Mather* (1891) remains one of the best studies of the "Puritan Priest." *English Composition* (1891) was reprinted into the 1940s and created the general pattern of freshman writing programs. *A Literary History of America* (1900), his best-known work, has been remembered merely as the conservative, anglophile, provincial history of New England literature; and it probably helped to solidify the professional attitude against American literature in the universities. But the *Literary History*, the beginning of serious attention to American literature, is unsympathetic toward the old heroes of New England literature; and it is positive about writers like Edgar Allan Poe, Nathaniel Hawthorne, Mark Twain, and especially Walt Whitman, despite the pressures of his Tory, aristocratic, conservative biases. Furthermore, Wendell's *History* is a cultural essay that attempts to trace with historical, theological, and aesthetic concerns the development of the American mind around his thesis of "American inexperience," his term for the concept of American innocence.

The purpose of this book is threefold: to describe Barrett Wendell the individual, to analyze in some detail his professional writings, and to survey the nature and influence of his teaching career at Harvard. Wendell's adult life coincided with some of the most tumultuous years of transition and expansion in American history, and the major emphasis of this book is an understanding of Wendell's life and work within the context of that rapidly changing time. Limitations of space preclude any in-depth commentary on the intellectual, cultural, and political history of the last three decades of the nineteenth century and the first two decades of this century. However, a general historical overview is presented in the first chapter, and more specific, albeit brief, descriptions of background are provided as appropriate or necessary in subsequent chapters. Little more than general comparisons are made between Wendell's critical theories and values and similar concerns of his contemporaries or successors in order to focus primarily on the specific nature and import of his extensive writings.

The first chapter seeks to find among biographical data the "temperamental facts" of Wendell's life, whereas the second chapter analyzes those same facts as reflected in his study of Cotton Mather.

The third chapter attempts to define the social and political views presupposed in Wendell's literary studies and expressed specifically in *Liberty, Union, and Democracy; The France of Today;* and *The Privileged Classes.* The fourth chapter analyzes the theories and the form of his literary histories: *William Shakspere, The Temper of the Seventeenth Century in English Literature*, and *The Traditions of European Literature.* With this background of Wendell's social, political, and literary perspectives, the fifth and sixth chapters analyze his major work, *A Literary History of America.* The seventh chapter describes Wendell the teacher, his official role at Harvard, and the extent of his influence on students and colleagues. Finally, chapter 8 looks at Wendell's career in terms of the negative assessments accorded his work in the twentieth century.

Personally and professionally Wendell felt that he lacked the courage, the strength, and the temperament to accept change; but he also felt the need to confront the vast change in his own day. George Santayana's definition of the Genteel Tradition describes a paradigm which we discover throughout Wendell's career: "America is not simply . . . a young country with an old mentality: it is a country with two mentalities, one a survival of the beliefs and standards of the fathers, the other an expression of the instincts, practice, and discoveries of the younger generations."[1] Wendell's life, his habits, his teaching, and his criticism reflect the ambivalence of a man caught between two such mentalities, between two eras. Wendell's work is flawed by his double vision, but it is the purpose of this study to delineate the strengths as well as the often-noted weakness of that work and to present the transitional figure whose work actively helped to enfranchise the literary rebellion of the twentieth century against the nineteenth; whose voice helped to prepare the way for American literature of the twentieth century.

ROBERT T. SELF

Northern Illinois University

Acknowledgments

I wish to express my gratitude especially to C. Carroll Hollis, of the University of North Carolina, whose knowledge and understanding first awakened my interest in this period of American literature; who first introduced me to Barrett Wendell and encouraged me in this project; and who provided invaluable insight and criticism in the early stages of its development. Robert Bain and William Powers read the early manuscript and gave me important suggestions for additions and revisions. The late Barrett Wendell II shared with me personal recollections of his father; and I wish to thank Mr. F. Lee H. Wendell and the Barrett Wendell estate for permission to quote from Wendell's letters, lectures, and manuscripts. I must also thank the staff of the Houghton Library and the archives at Harvard University, of the Butler Library at Columbia University, and of the New York Public Library for assistance in studying the letters and papers of Barrett Wendell. I am grateful to the University of North Carolina for two Smith Fund grants and to Northern Illinois University for a grant from the Council of Academic Deans that enabled me to complete the research for this project. Sylvia Bowman's advice on the structure and revision of the final manuscript has been of utmost importance. And finally I wish to thank my wife Lois whose knowledge of American intellectual history and whose patience and support provided the greatest assistance and encouragement of all.

Chronology

1855   Barrett Wendell born August 23 in Boston.
1863   Moved to New York.
1872   Entered Harvard College; suffered nervous breakdown.
1873   Reentered Harvard.
1876   Helped found the *Harvard Lampoon.*
1877   Graduated from Harvard; entered Harvard Law School.
1878–   Student of law in New York firm of Anderson and Howland.
1879
1879–   Student of law in Boston firm of Shattuck, Holmes, and Mun-
1880   roe.
1880   Failed Massachusetts bar examination; married Edith Greenough; appointed instructor in English at Harvard.
1884   Initiated new writing program at Harvard with A. S. Hill and LeBaron Briggs; began teaching English 12, Elective Composition.
1885   Published his first novel, *The Duchess Emilia;* succeeded Hill as instructor in English 5, Advanced Composition; helped found *The Harvard Monthly.*
1886   Elected to Phi Beta Kappa.
1887   Published his second novel, *Rankell's Remains;* uproar in Boston papers over Mugwump sympathies in the book.
1888   Promoted to assistant professor.
1889   Elected fellow of the American Academy of Arts and Sciences.
1890   Elected Trustee of the Boston Athenaeum; delivered Lowell Institute lectures, "English Composition."
1891   Published *Cotton Mather* and *English Composition.*
1892   Began teaching English 23, Shakespeare.
1893   Published *Stelligeri.*
1894   Published *Shakspere.*

1896–	Chairman of the Harvard English Department.
1901	
1897	Began teaching English 20, Research in the Literary History of America.
1898	Promoted to Professor of English; began English 33, Literary History of America, offered continuously until his retirement.
1900	Published *A Literary History of America*.
1901	Lecturer at the University of California.
1902	Published *Ralegh in Guiana*, poetry and drama in the "Elizabethan manner."
1902–	Delivered Clark Lectures, Trinity College in Cambridge
1903	University on seventeenth-century English literature; represented Harvard at the Tercentenary of the Bodleian Libary in Oxford.
1904	Began teaching Comparative Literature I, European Literature from Homer to Dante; published the school edition of the *Literary History: A History of Literature in America;* published *The Temper of the Seventeenth Century in English Literature;* helped initiate the honors degree in history and literature; served as chairman of the program until his retirement.
1904–	Delivered Hyde Foundation lectures at the Sorbonne in
1905	Paris, "American Ideals and Institutions," as the first exchange professor to France.
1905	Published *Selections from the Writings of Joseph Addison;* delivered Lowell Institute lectures, "National Ideals of America."
1906	Published *Liberty, Union, and Democracy;* delivered Lowell Institute lectures, "Impressions of Contemporary France."
1907	Published *The France of Today*.
1908	Published *The Privileged Classes;* uproar in Boston, New York, and Chicago in the press and among labor against the book's aristocratic description of the working man.
1909	Published *The Mystery of Education*.
1910	French translation of *The France of Today* published.
1913	Received honorary Doctor of Letters degree from Columbia University.
1914	Offered lectureship, similar to the Sorbonne lectures, at the University of Berlin.

1916   Elected to American Academy of Arts and Letters.
1917   Retired in June to become professor emeritus.
1918   Received honorary Doctor of Letters degree from Harvard University.
1920   Published *The Traditions of European Literature;* received honorary Doctor of Laws degree from University of Strasburg in France; elected to the Board of Overseers, Harvard.
1921   Death of Wendell on February 8.

CHAPTER 1

The Amber of Irony

THE handbooks of literary history tell us that Barrett Wendell (1855–1921) taught English at Harvard from 1880 to 1917; that he wrote the influential rhetoric text *English Composition* (1891), one of the best biographies of Cotton Mather (1891), and one of the major studies of American literature, *A Literary History of America* (1900); that he was the first American exchange lecturer at the Sorbonne (1904–1905); that he gained French and American acclaim for his study of prewar France (1906); and that he was famous to four generations of Harvard students as the aristocratic, eccentric, and challenging professor of creative writing, American literature, and comparative literature; and that he was the last of the Cambridge Brahmins.

I *American History*

Barrett Wendell was born August 5, 1855; his life and career exactly describe a major period of transition not only in American literature but also in American history. In 1865, when Wendell was ten years old, the United States emerged from the conflict of fratricidal war a nation of thirty-two million with few states west of the Mississippi, its government and economy in chaos, its president assassinated. By 1921, when Wendell died at the age of sixty-six, there were forty-eight states with a population of one hundred six million; the ruined old South had become the New South growing with industry and the Ku Klux Klan; the trans-Mississippi frontier was the closed, tamed Great West. Millions of European and Asian immigrants had flooded to both shores. The small provincial nation of 1855 had survived civil war and embarked on imperialism in the Pacific and the Caribbean. Sectional enmity had given way to national unity in face of the German Hun, and the United States had emerged as one of the great world powers.

In politics, during Wendell's life, a succession of mostly Republican presidents gave the reins of government over to laissez-faire economics, to corruption, and to machine politics like New York's Tammany Hall. Sectional interests generated angry actions and rhetoric in the Greenback Party, the Free Silver issue, the Granger and Populist movements. And, by the end of this period, the trust-busting, jingoist energy of Wendell's friend "Rough Rider" Teddy Roosevelt was supplanted by the Fourteen Points, the international outlook of Woodrow Wilson, and the proposal of a League of Nations. One of the outstanding phenomena of the age was the invention of the corporation and the trust, the rise of big-business capitalism. Railroads, steel, and oil made huge fortunes for the Rockefellers, the Mellons, the Carnegies who employed the dynamo, the steam engine, and the wealth of America's natural resources to catapult the United States into the forefront as the greatest industrial nation in the world, to ruin thousands of acres of land and water, and to create an exploited and impoverished laboring class. American know-how invented the telephone, the electric light, the automobile, the motion picture, and in the 1890s the worst economic crises in the national history. Meanwhile, the initial organizing efforts of labor led to strikes, widespread violence, and the fear shared by Wendell of anarchists and communism.

In religion, the decades of Wendell's life were equally varied and turbulent. On the level of eastern aristocracy, Calvinism with its dogma of the depravity of man and the predestined election to salvation by God's grace had developed in two ways. Earlier in the nineteenth century it had evolved, on one hand, into the beliefs of Unitarianism which demoted Jesus from the Trinity and made him a Good Man; and it subsequently evolved into the liberal, idealistic philosophy of transcendentalism, which posited man's power to intuit through nature not a traditional God but the oversoul and the essential unity of all man. By the late nineteenth century, the religion of Ralph Waldo Emerson had degenerated into a complacent and liberal Anglicanism or agnosticism. On the other hand, Puritanism's concept of election developed through the preachments of Benjamin Franklin into an American dream, or myth, of success.

In novel after novel Horatio Alger inculcated the possibility that every shoeshine boy with industry and thrift might achieve financial and moral success; and the work of C. S. Peirce and William James gave intellectual respectability to this American energy in the philosophy of pragmatism: if it works, it's true. Religion and science were at great odds over the nature of man; but, by the end of the century Charles Darwin's biological theory of evolution and Herbert Spencer's synthetic philosophy of the mechanistic evolution of the cosmos were merged with religious and capitalist views to defend the Gospel of Wealth. Struggle meant competition; survival of the fittest meant economic success; evolution meant progress to bigger and better things.

Social Darwinism is a major paradigm for the intellectual, religious, social, political, and economic life of the late nineteenth century. In Spencer's view, the forces of evolution and dissolution worked together in rhythm as life moved inexorably from homogeneous, or simple, forms to heterogeneous, or complex ones, and toward greater sophistication, greater stability, greater coherence of matter. Societally, the "laws" of Darwin and Spencer were argued, feared, damned; but they fostered a belief in efficacious reform, improvement, progress, utopia. Yet contrary to the faith in social betterment, men like William Graham Sumner, Brooks Adams, Henry Adams, and Barrett Wendell reacted pessimistically to evolution: as life developed, it consumed more and more irreplaceable energy. They interpreted evolution in light of the laws of thermodynamics to mean that energy and life were running down; and the longer the evolutionary progression the greater the entropy, the greater would be the dissipation of energy. Evolution, to them, indicated not progress and hope but decay and despair.

In the arts, as well, the same energy, the same confusions, the same change and conflict obtained. Specifically in literature the nineteenth-century writers were romantic, then realistic, then naturalistic. In 1855, when Henry Wadsworth Longfellow published *Hiawatha* and Walt Whitman *Leaves of Grass*, American literature professed an interest in a divine oversoul, in human rights, in the love of nature, in individualism and freedom of expression, and, most significantly, in the preeminence of the creative imagination. But the reality of civil war and the pressures of a fast-paced, material life in the 1870s and 1880s led to the battle for realism fought by William Dean Howells, Hamlin Garland, and others against the sentimental, emotional excesses of romanticism. Such realists wanted fidelity to actual experience, to the logic of everyday life, to the objective surfaces of life for the "divine average," as well as a decorous presentation of the smiling aspects of American life that could be read by the teenage schoolgirl. The battle between romanticism and realism was waged in the pages of a new and vital medium: the large, mass magazines. While Howells championed realism, editors of magazines like *Atlantic Monthly*, *Scribner's,* and *Century* in the 1870s and 1880s spoke in concert for the Genteel Tradition.

The Genteel Tradition comprised the cultural standards of artists, critics, and editors like Edmund Clarence Stedman, Richard Henry Stoddard, George Henry Boker, Richard Watson Gilder, and Charles Eliot Norton. They were cultural missionaries and highly influential dictators of public taste who promoted the prestige of art and whose normal rectitude promoted a "feminization" of literary decorum. They expressed a romantic appreciation for ideality, not reality; for the serene and the beautiful; for the moral with a high sense of craft; for the novels of Thomas Bailey Aldrich, not John W. DeForest; for the poetry of James Whitcomb Riley, not the sexual degeneracy and formlessness of Walt Whitman. In pre–Civil War America, the Cambridge and Concord writers constituted a cultured, intellectual elite, a philosophical and literary upper class which enjoyed prestige unprecedented thereafter, but to which Genteel editors and critics felt themselves heir. Most of these critics were late nineteenth-century Brahmins (from Oliver Wendell Holmes's famous definition of the New England aristocracy), who clung to the increasingly outmoded idealism and humanism of Emerson, Longfellow, James R. Lowell and who longed anachronistically for their same kind of cultural authority. By the end of the century, both the realists and idealists found a common enemy in naturalism, a sordid, pessimistic import from France that upheld scientific objectivity, frankness, amorality, and the belief that man was governed not by reason, will, or imagination but by the external forces of heredity and environment.

The last two decades of Wendell's life echoed with critical blasts against the repressive values of the Genteel Tradition; and Wendell at Harvard, George Woodberry at Columbia, and Henry Van Dyke at Princeton were being charged as coconspirators with the Genteel editors for serving up to America a sterile heritage—for denying its youth a viable American past with which to encounter the moral, political, aesthetic demands of a new century. Van Wyck Brooks called for a unified culture in opposition to the nineteenth-century separation of highbrow aristocracy and lowbrow philistinism. Joel Spingarn described the new criticism in which art has a life of its own, with no connection to morality; and Irving Babbitt preached a new humanism of classical authority, universal truth, and morality of personal discipline.

The fantastic crosscurrents of literary modes and critical values between 1855 and 1921 are reflected in the major artists of the period: Holmes, John Greenleaf Whittier, Longfellow, Lowell, Emerson, Hawthorne, Whitman, James, Howells, Stephen Crane, Theodore Dreiser. If Richard Watson Gilder, Richard Henry Stoddard, and Hamilton Wright Mabie pointed the way to the neoromantic mood prior to World War I—expressed in works like Charles Major's *When Knighthood Was in Flower*, O'Henry's *Four Million*, and Zane Grey's *Riders of the Purple Sage*—William Dean Howells and Henry James helped significantly to carry American critical thought from romantic impressionism to a high sense of aesthetic craftsmanship. And if Dreiser's *Sister Carrie* was too strong in 1900 for the editor Doubleday, by 1921, when Wendell died, the modern revolution in American literature, the second renaissance, was well underway in the work of Robert Frost, Ezra Pound, T. S. Eliot, Eugene O'Neill, F. Scott Fitzgerald, and Sinclair Lewis.

II *A Biography*

Against this historical background, we seek to understand Barrett Wendell, who as we might expect of a Brahmin was born in Boston. His earliest ancestors were Dutch traders who settled in New York in the 1640s, but most of his ancestral ties were in Massachusetts and New Hampshire. The Wendell family had been merchants and traders, though his paternal grandmother was descended from a New England governor, a Harvard president, and the Puritan divine John Rogers. Wendell's grandfather had made a fortune as a privateer during the War of 1812 but had subsequently failed in shipping and manufacturing endeavors. His father Jacob was born in poverty, but his Yankee industry came to fruition after ten years with J. C. Howe and Company, Boston and New York agents for cottons and woolens, when he was made a partner in the firm, which eventually became Jacob Wendell and Company. The Wendell family moved to New York City in 1863 when young Barrett was eight years old, an important business move for his father, but one which began Wendell's lifelong distaste for the city of his earliest American ancestors. He wrote years later in his memoir: "Compared with Boston, I can now see, it was surging with growth, which means incessant change; and change I have never found instantly sympathetic."[1]

His youth was spent in affluent respectability. Though reared an Anglican, he displeased his parents from an early age with his religious attitudes; by 1880, he said, "my religious views had become, as they have on the whole remained, tolerantly agnostic, with sympathy for any honest faith, and an intellectual admiration for the logic of the Catholic Church" (120). His lifelong love for "Longfellow's Europe" began with his first visit to the Old World with his family in 1868, and his admiration for English literature dated from a gift in the same period of a complete set of William Thackeray's novels, works beyond his years but the first impulse toward a career in belles lettres. At the age of ten, too, he used to watch the popular Massachusetts sculptor John Rogers as he worked; without exposure to the "sheer force" of Rogers's "creative imagination," Wendell wrote later, "I might not have come instinctively to understand that the final test of fine art is to be found in its own inherent beauty" (65).

For the most part, Wendell's education was private, and the most important readings he encountered were the *Aeneid*, the *Bucolics*, and the *Georgics*, works from a tradition that provided him pleasure and critical touchstones his whole life. He made his second journey to Europe in 1871, but the main object of his attention then was Harvard. Wendell felt continually the pressure of his father's expectations for him, and this pressure might have accounted for a nervous breakdown in his freshman year in Cambridge. From his youth, Wendell was never strong; and he attributed his nervous disability to a genetic inheritance from three generations in his father's family. He also injured his back in his teens, so that walking was painful and necessitated the use of his famous and often caricatured cane. His breakdown from "hysterical paralysis" in 1872 became the occasion for a year's journey abroad to Africa, Asia, and Europe, from which he returned to Harvard and the class of 1877. His college career was distinguished neither academically nor socially, but he wrote for the *Crimson* and contributed significantly to the newly formed *Lampoon*. The greatest influence of these years, as we shall see, was the tutelage in classics of James Russell Lowell, then at the end of his Harvard career.

Following Wendell's graduation, he entered the Harvard Law School and the next year read law with the firm of Anderson and Howland in New York; in 1879–1880, he read in the law offices of Shattuck, Holmes (Oliver Wendell, Jr.), and Munroe. But 1880 was the momentous year for Wendell. He failed the bar examination, married Edith Greenough of a prominent Boston family, and received a desperately needed job offer: a telegram from Harvard proposed a position as a theme reader under his old professor Adams Sherman Hill. Wendell wrote in his memoirs: "The telegram decided my career; it also gratified my father as indicating, for the first time, that somebody thought me conceivably useful. Though I began teaching at Harvard thus fortuitously and with no notion of keeping it up long, and though more than once I came near dropping the work, I was actually on the roles there as a teacher for thirty-seven years" (109). Although we survey his illustrious career, during one of Harvard's golden eras, in chapter 8, Wendell's position was not for many years a secure one; this fact is evident from his repeatedly defensive attitude toward the new doctoral-degree orientation and from his consternation at being promoted to full professor some twenty years after joining the faculty. He became an assistant professor in 1888, but his career nearly ended in 1893 when he clashed with Harvard Overseer Bishop Phillips Brooks. Brooks was a close friend of Wendell's brother Evert, and for some reason, as Wendell reported in his memoir, the bishop "presently conceived me to be a dangerous influence for undergraduates; and a year before I was to come up for reappointment as assistant professor, President Eliot privately told me that Brooks, as an overseer, would oppose me, and that my value to the College was hardly such as to warrent controversy with so good a man" (142–43). However, Wendell noted succinctly, Brooks died first.

If only by accident an academician, Wendell expressed his political interests from the early 1880s. In 1884, he supported the Mugwump revolt from the Republican party. He came under heavy attack from Boston newspapers for what to them seemed a malicious description in his novel *Rankell's Remains* of the Republican convention that nominated James G. Blaine. In that same year, he witnessed with enthusiasm the Democratic convention that nominated Grover Cleveland in Chicago where Wendell was proctoring Harvard admissions examinations. There he not only conversed with William Graham Sumner about the independent movement in Connecticut but was grilled by Blaine's son about Wendell's failure to support his father. Wendell's early political involvement seems to have been liberal if not totally active. He once remarked that, had he stayed in New York, he might have become a Tammany man; and he asserted in 1892 to his father, in opposition to Republican economic measures like the McKinley Tariff, "I am for the moment a blind democrat."[2]

Whether because of the uncertainty of his reappointment at Harvard with his fourth child on the way, some financial setback in the panic of 1893, or the general economic disasters of Cleveland's second administration, Wendell's social and political views became increasingly conservative and often despairing after 1893. In 1896, he voted for the Republican from Ohio, William McKinley, and a straight Republican ticket for the first time. He did not participate in the academically popular Anti-Imperialist League; indeed, he extolled Theodore Roosevelt as a new American hero who, with high position, stressed not privilege or equality but opportunity. Yet when he and Brooks Adams spent some days in 1912 with Roosevelt following his announcement to run against William Howard Taft for the Republican nomination, Wendell wrote to his daughter Mary that Roosevelt "seems to me dangerous, having steadily tended toward radical extreme; but then, no one seems safe. I feel as if social revolution were near, probably inevitable."[3] And he equally feared Woodrow Wilson's "doctrinarian socialism."

These later conservative, even reactionary views, as we shall see, underlie much of his literary, political, and social writings from 1900 until his death. They did not, however, prevent him from becoming one of the most prominent academicians of his day. Not only was he intimate with many of the leading contemporary figures—William Dean Howells, Brooks and Henry Adams, Abbott Lawrence Lowell, William James, Theodore Roosevelt, Henry Cabot Lodge—but his own views were well known through widespread book, magazine, and newspaper dissemination. He spoke regularly at conferences and universities around the country—in California, Missouri, Texas, South Carolina, Virginia, New York. Continuing his European travels, he lectured at Cambridge University in 1902–1903 and in France at the Sorbonne in 1904–1905. When he toured the world in 1910–1911, he was received at the royal courts of Asia. His retirement dinner in June, 1917, was an occasion as momentous as the 1912 Howells tribute in New York. After retirement, he continued to write and lecture, publishing his last work the year before his death February 8, 1921.

III *Temperamental Facts*

Such facts indicate something of the public Barrett Wendell, but little of the man that he and subsequent critics felt him to be; they do not explain why his former student, Princeton drama professor Walter Eaton, could write in the 1924 *American Mercury:* "I have never been able to persuade . . . the Twentieth Century that Barrett Wendell was a great man." He also noted that Wendell's influence faded before his death and that "in another generation will perhaps be forgotten, unless some biographer . . . enshrines him in the amber of irony."[4] This last phrase sets very well the tenor of our attempt to delineate the "temperamental" facts of Barrett Wendell's life, for his whole career is marked by irony and paradox. Though a success in his own time, Wendell felt his career a failure; and the twentieth-century interpretation of the man has concurred superficially in that judgment because of its distaste for Wendell's Puritan predilections, his aristocratic and conservative defense of the "wrong" American tradition, his Brahmin unhappiness with democratic equality, and his failure to recognize the "true" American artists of the nineteenth century. Such negative readings of Wendell's life are narrow, because they derive on the one hand from the early twentieth century's rejection of nineteenth-century values which seemed irrelevant in the chaotic, post–World War I years and on the other hand from an inability to see with clarity and objectivity the historical perspectives of Wendell's life and work.

Stuart Sherman wrote of Wendell's "paradoxical" life: "I find the most important tokens of Wendell's humanity not in his fortunate and effective and happy external career but in the series of his failures and in the record of impulses which bore little fruit."[5] Like Henry Adams, his worth lies in his tragic qualities; and his "success" rests in part on his representation of the late nineteenth-century efforts to maintain the old traditions in terms of a world in the midst of sad and turbulent change. H. L. Mencken aptly described the man, his problem, and its results: "Sentimentally and emotionally, he was moved powerfully by the New England tradition, and felt a strong impulse to defend it against the world. Intellectually, he saw clearly that it was in collapse around him—worse, that it had been full of defects and weaknesses even when, by his own doctrine, it had been strong. The result was his endless shuttling between worship and ribaldry."[6] In a letter to a friend in 1904, Wendell himself sounded a tragic note in a striking metaphor: "There was never

a more queer career than this solitary, blind one of mine, flapping
wings skyward through mists which distract my eyes, and those that
look at me as well."[7] Echoed again in his own epitaph—"he lacked
the courage to do good or evil"—this tragic quality is in a sense
Prufrockian; it reveals a man for whom "talking of Michelangelo" is a
lost art from the old culture and also a man awakened by human
voices of a new century. Like T. S. Eliot's Prufrock, he was often
odd, eccentric, absurd; and he was painfully aware of those traits.

Wendell lamented in 1893, "I feel a certain regret that I had not
the fortune to be born fifty years earlier. Then I could eagerly have
joined in the expression of faith in the future which made New
England literature promise something."[8] In the 1890s, however, he
could not "force the moment to its crisis." In a letter to Robert
Herrick he described himself as "wishing to goodness that at your
time of life I had had at once the luck and pluck to give and take in a
world where something was a-doing. Masculinity isn't my trait,
now, I fear; so I love the trait far more than it may be worth by the
standard of the eternities."[9] Wendell constantly conceived the need
for the vigorous life in a time when old values clashed with new; yet
his life presents us with another portrait of a man uncertain about
both value systems. No less than Henry Adams's pose of diffidence
and failure, Wendell's habitual role of unsympathetic Tory was a
defense against uncertainty: his failure may at least be described as a
successful protest against the pressure of his heritage and his personal sense of inadequacy.

Yet the major irony is that, while Wendell felt himself out of joint
with the new spirit in American culture, he was inextricably bound
up in that transition between old and new; he was a product of that
transition, indeed a prime example of the debilitation caused by
major transitional periods; and, at the same time, he was one of the
forces that sped the coming revolution to arms. These general observations provide us with broad limits within which to describe the
life of a man who lived outside his time and who represents that
time, a man who championed aesthetic excellence and humanistic
taste, a man of uncertain faith teaching at a university which produced so many modern tastemakers and whose association with
James Russell Lowell was no more important than his influence on
Amy Lowell.

Stuart Sherman shuddered to think how the new historian would
deal with such a man: "What sort of caricature would our treacher-

ous memories and our still more treacherous 'realistic methods' "
produce? Sherman feared "some quite inadequate statement of his
idiosyncracy," touched up with Wendell's "abundant external ec-
centricities,"[10] and subsequent commentary on the Harvard professor have borne out these fears. Charles F. Thwing, president of
Case Western Reserve University, remembered Wendell with the
whitewash of sentimentality as a man of faith in the eternal verities.
George Santayana wondered how much his colleague, benefactor,
and former teacher was a fool and how much a martyr. And, as late
as 1966, Martin Green reiterated the superficial clichés: "When one
thinks of Wendell's general cynicism, and general dissatisfaction
with American morality, one would prefer to think him insincere
[on the "purity of Life" in America] . . . . But it is more likely to
have been the result of sheer muddle in his mind."[11]

The man thus remembered—consummate Tory, prejudiced New
Englander, despairing critic of American life and letters—was not
the man, in the words of Robert Herrick, "who will be remembered
by students and colleagues and friends as a singularly lovable and
unusual personality," and remembered for "just those pet ideas of
class, those political and social beliefs which meant least, not to
himself but to those who recognized the man beneath the arabesque
of temperamental opinion in which he delighted to drape himself in
endless improvisation."[12]

Wendell's facetious, but prophetic self-description at twenty-
four—"handsome, accomplished, genial, beautiful, foolish, studi-
ous, literary, sentimental, and unhappy"—illustrates both the truth
about Wendell and those glaring contrasts of his life which led Abbott Lawrence Lowell to quote Wendell's words about James Russell Lowell as self-revealing: "There was the real man, and what he
thought himself to be; and the former was the larger."[13]

IV *Unsettled Relations*

It is significant that, while William Dean Howells made a symbol-
ically meaningful move to New York in the 1880s, Wendell left New
York for Boston and Harvard. While the growing nation moved
steadily westward, Wendell never left what he called the "sterile"
Boston influence. Indeed, the sudden dislocation of his youth in
moving to booming New York "helps explain the often imperfect
serenity of my atmospheric reactions and diffusions." While Howells seemed always trying to embrace the future, Wendell super-

ficially seemed intent on capturing the past. Something, of course, in this eastward-turning tendency characterized a large part of the self-conscious American mind; yet, if it is true in this case that, as an old order changes, its defenders resort to breeding, then Wendell more closely approximates one of the generalizations about the Genteel Tradition. As an antiquarian who resurrected the family coat of arms, collected Copley portraits of his ancestors, restored the old family home in Portsmouth, New Hampshire, and proudly found relatives in the New England Holmeses, Wentworths, Quincys, and Phillips, Wendell has appeared as a man unable to see the forest for the family trees. President Eliot felt that "Wendell's frequent discourse on the subject of birth and descent seems snobbish in an American, and will cause many to underestimate his judgment and good sense."[14]

Yet, ironically, Wendell's breeding, his impressive ancestry, never produced security. His father's business success made Wendell equally insecure though it explains perhaps Wendell's impulse to seek an older, safer aristocracy. Jacob Wendell was a successful, commanding personality; and Wendell never felt he had matched his father's expectations. His many trips to Europe were financed by his father, who also purchased Wendell's Boston home in Marlborough Street. "At heart," Wendell wrote, "I still think of myself as troublesomely poor and indulge my frequent comforts with a disquieting sense of impudence in hot guilt." Wendell's son recalled Wendell's feeling of financial inadequacy that led the son to assume all his father's business affairs and to maintain them in secrecy because of the extreme nervousness that accompanied Wendell's awareness of any movement up or down in a bond. Wendell often indicated unhappiness with his own career, and his sense of financial uncertainty entwined clearly with his relationship to his own father: "At sixty-three I have never displayed the economic powers for which he ever so buoyantly hoped" (18, 126).

Wendell's family life revealed his need for "a settled relation to my surroundings . . . ; and separation from domestic authority deeply affectionate and yet incessantly irritating." In his *Literary History*, his observations of Henry David Thoreau are telling as to his own perspectives: Thoreau "had the good sense not to marry; and as nobody was dependent on him for support, his method of life could do no harm."[15] Barrett Wendell, Jr., remembered that his mother was by far the stronger of the two, and that his father leaned on her for everything. His insecurity about finances and domestic relations compounded Wendell's physical weakness; colleagues recalled that nervous prostration was a constant problem and that he frequently seemed the victim of moods. At the age of twenty-four he wrote despairingly to Fred Stimson: "My life is a succession of fits of indignation at my own weakness, and fits of complete *abandon* to that weakness, in which I grow weaker and weaker . . . ; I am beginning to fear . . . that while man proposed that I should be something, God in his infinite wisdom is disposing of me as a mere copyist in a bad hand—with an ultimate view to the fertilization of the soil."[16] His weakness and sense of failure must also have been accentuated by his younger brother Evert, an intercollegiate track star, a success in their father's business, and a famous philanthropist.

Forever vacillating between a psychological need for calm and a mental need for action produced in Wendell the puzzling, conservative character who would suddenly startle a class, a dinner audience, or an official Harvard with an obscenity and created a split personality dismissed as eccentric by critics, explained as superficial by friends, and cited by way of excuse by Wendell himself. He protected himself from serious responsibility for spoken judgments by pointing out his "temperamental misfortune to express myself in a manner which has appeared frivolous," and he claimed that his "desultory and excessive mental habits would in any case have prevented me from figuring as much of a scholar."

Comparing himself in 1906 to his friend Senator Lodge, "a man who has known the stress of life," he felt the difference to be that "between real experience and quasi-histrionic admiration thereof." In an attitude little recognized by his critics, Wendell reacted against the "fastidious over-refinement" in contemporary literature and also defined the irony and tragedy of his own life:

To come from this [robust literature of the sixteenth century] to the self-analytic inaction of the nineteenth century is shocking. And I, for one, cannot quite feel, at all events in this great, growing America of ours, that this introspection, this idealistic inaction, is really a necessity; and certainly it is not to me an ideal. A man who goes through life without playing an active part is a failure. He may be a noble one; but his life is real tragedy. . . . Action is the ideal we should keep before us—an active struggle with the life we are born to, a full sense of all its temptations, of all its earthly significance as well as of its spiritual.[17]

As the crudeness of a Gilded Age threatened the solid virtues of old New England, Wendell's affirmation of social virility, his nervous weakness, and his sense of financial insecurity help explain Wendell's ambivalent character—one that looked backward and forward and expressed itself sharply, iconoclastically, conservatively, doubtfully. Even as an undergraduate these same traits appear: "Perhaps still in a somewhat 'cocky' and snobbish fashion, which prevented his attaining the social success achieved there by football captains, he was an iconoclast, an enemy of Philistinism, and, significantly, a founder of the 'Harvard Lampoon.' "[18] His contributions to the early years of that publication helped give it a reputation outside of college circles, and his character Hollis Alworthy—a stereotype for some years of the dapper, sophisticated, superficial Harvard aristocrat—reveals Wendell's Brahmin interests and an ironic perspective toward that attitude: "Hollis Alworthy is not aware that his ancestors have ever been sufficiently in sympathy with popular movements to achieve much public distinction. But . . . for more than two hundred years every one of them has been a graduate of Harvard."[19]

In later years, Wendell himself became a subject of the *Lampoon*, especially for his appearance which revealed an ostentatious, affected, disdainful self-consciousness. Many students have recalled his physical appearance as unique among professors because of his unacademic, fashionable, English-looking clothes and spats. But part of that fashion was eccentric and affected. He had a highly exaggerated English accent and spoke in what Mencken called a "whinnying voice." Santayana's curiosity led him to wonder, "*why* did Barrett Wendell talk like that?" His answer is instructive: "He would have wished to be a Cavalier, all courage and elegance. His speech was a failure as a mark of elegance but it was a success as a proof of courage. Anyhow, it was a profound constant protest against being like other people."[20]

Wendell himself maintained that, if he were to meet himself, he would detest his own personal appearance and find his own voice and manner irritating "like perverse affections." The contrast here between a cultivated self-image and a distaste for that image reveals again the man caught between a need for assertiveness and a doubt of his assets, and it might explain much about the man whose favorite hobby was amateur theatrics (he wrote and played in Elizabethan verse dramas)—the histrionic Wendell whose deportment showed that he was acting much of the time.

V *"Queerly out of it"*

The need for such acting might easily have arisen from the pattern of failure marking his early manhood; certainly it reinforced his sense of weakness and insecurity. He was the first of the Holmes's law firm to fail his bar examinations; he tried his hand at novels and quit after two when he and his reviewers agreed that he lacked talent; and, like his younger brother Jacob, he attempted to be a serious dramatist but with no success. His long career at Harvard began by a chance conversation with his old rhetoric teacher Hill and continued because he had been unable to break into the life of his times at any other point, not because he wanted to spend his lifetime teaching, especially at Harvard where the highly professional historical and philological studies of George Lyman Kittredge set an enviable standard. Wendell's only degree was the Bachelor of Arts; and, with the proliferation of Germanic scholarship and graduate education, he was forever exclaiming, "God knows I am no scholar!" In his books, he excused his theories as the effort of a "mere man of letters." In his classes, he would begin by describing himself as more dilettante than scientist. In Paris, while lecturing at the Sorbonne, he felt "queerly out of it academically," a feeling he was familiar with at Harvard where his sense of insecurity must have grown as promotion to professor was withheld until eighteen years following his first appointment.

Santayana, who finally had the strength to leave Harvard, was never quite happy there either; and he called Wendell, like himself, one of the "stray souls" in official Harvard. And Stuart Sherman wrote:

I suppose Harvard is as "free" a university as there is in the country, and only men who have worked there can know how unfree the freest university is, how oppressively it constrains all but the most potent spirits to conform to its type. Barrett Wendell, like William James was, or became, a potent spirit, and both men were indulged rebels in Cambridge. It is the glory of Harvard that, though she laughs at her rebels and lets them understand that rebellion can never be taken seriously, she does indulge them.[21]

What must official indulgence have meant to a man with the desires and fears that Wendell brought to his teaching? He speaks with knowledgeable sympathy in his literary history of the unhappiness of Longfellow and Lowell at Harvard, and we do not wonder that such a man increasingly longed for a time when merely being a teacher gained entrance into the Boston aristocracy and when teaching required no scientific training.

His efforts at creative writing reveal an equally debilitating attitude. In 1880, he wrote that "it is maddening to have to do one's best work in an amateurish way, if not actually on the sly—at the risk of having fingers pointed at you if you are found out." In itself, to write creatively was a means of attacking and avoiding the scientific scholarship he detested; but his first two books, *The Duchess Emilia* (1885) and *Rankell's Remains* (1887), did little to enhance Wendell's standing in his department. Though one novel gained notoriety, they reveal little artistic merit—weak characterization in Gothic plots, inane dialogue, superficial description, and confused point of view. Realizing, as he told Edmund Clarence Stedman, that "literature is evidently not to be my staff in life," he turned to more scholarly matters and worked very hard on *Cotton Mather* and *English Composition*. Academically, he was rewarded; for he wrote Stedman in 1892 that the Mather book, "distinctly successful," "has done for me what my novels never began to do, in making people take what I do seriously."[22] But at what price? Wendell applauded E. A. Robinson's artistic integrity and escape from Harvard, but his own creative writing went underground.

Wendell's friends were aware that he always intended to write another novel, but how deeply his creative endeavors ran is not clear from the small volume of Elizabethan-style plays he published or from his two magazine short stories. His manuscript writings include eight plays, nine short stories, some tentative chapters of a projected novel, and two stories translated from the French. Such evidence clearly corroborates the testimony of former students that the greatness of Wendell's teaching derived from the fact that he was at heart an artist; and that he was a frustrated artist is an even greater certainty. If one wanted to write novels, Wendell later advised his students, one should stick to it. He urged them to be more courageous with their imaginations than he had been. If not defensively, Wendell nonetheless covers his frustrated creativity with characteristic wit in the preface to *The Mystery of Education* (1909):

> Poeta nasitur non fit
> And that's the very deuce of it.

VI   *The Active Life*

Wendell produced a prodigious amount of writing, ranging from an attack on merging Harvard with Radcliffe to a report on the "Government of Jamaica, 1867–1901." Merely to list it, from his first novel in 1885 to his large volume on traditions in European literature, would consume several pages. Separating the truth, the honesty, the prejudice, and the error from this work and ascertaining the validity of Santayana's observation that Wendell was a good critic of undergraduate essays but not a fair historian or a learned man—these are our concern in subsequent chapters. His writing, however, indicates both his energy and the scope of his interests, ranging through interpretive biographies, literary histories, composition texts, political philosophy, and social theory. At his death, he had finished the first volume of *The Traditions of European Literature* (1920) and was at work on the second. In addition to these books, he wrote memoirs, introductions to edited manuscripts, translations from Latin, an encyclopedia piece on the American temperament, and political observations on Japan. As to which of these writings is most important, critics have disagreed. Wendell himself felt *Cotton Mather* and *English Composition* to be his "most noteworthy literary feat," but *A Literary History of America* is the work with which Wendell has generally been associated and, as we shall see later, is the book which reveals best the limitations and strengths of Wendell's insights and methods.

However we may judge them today, these books, constantly reviewed and reprinted, gained Wendell an international reputation. *English Composition* replaced Hill's famous *Rhetoric* for many generations of college students. His *Literary History* and the high school text version were standards in American education for longer than his critics liked to remember. His aristocratic denunciation of the new privileged class, the working class in their demands for "representation without taxation," evoked widespread reaction in the press; in academic circles his article on coeducation caused as much controversy as his negative opinions on the newer scientific theories of education. Three times he lectured under the august auspices of the Lowell Institute; in 1902–1903 he gave the Clark Lectures at Trinity College, Cambridge; and he represented Harvard at the Oxford Bodleian Tercentenary ceremonies. In 1904–1905, he inaugurated with great success the Hyde Foundation Lectures at the Sorbonne, where he found it most gratifying to be taken seriously. His *France of Today* won widespread acclaim both at home and abroad, was warmly praised by Ambassador J. J. Jusserand, and was translated into French. The popular impact of the book in France and America prompted public-opinion-minded German officials to offer Wendell in the spring of 1914 a lectureship at the University of Berlin similar to the appointment in Paris.

VII *Success*

Thomas Beer has recorded examples of another Wendell, the well-known after-dinner speaker, who "amused a party at dinner in Cambridge by comparing Collis Huntington to Bronson Alcott," and the Wendell wit: "A writer in *Scribner's Magazine* tells us good taste is universal in France. Good taste is not even universal in heaven." The wit that asked if the smell of sulphur was present at the funeral of western railroad baron Huntington often shocked students and scandalized Boston society and made Wendell "an inevitable speaker at Harvard meetings and dinners."[23]

That many felt Wendell's work to be conceived and executed by an "after dinner mind" may explain why serious recognition came slowly to Wendell, or perhaps it was because Wendell was chiefly a teacher, not a curator or investigator, that his scholastic honors came to him late in life. As he grew older, Wendell grew more pessimistic not only about the national course but about the efficacy of his own work, which he emphatically felt to be nothing but secondary utterances from an "unaggressive freethinker." He found it difficult to believe the honors he received, and he responded to them with characteristic irony: "If you could imagine Franklin, Webster, Channing, Hawthorne, Phillips Brooks, and Billy Sunday rolled into one, and endowed with the self-complacency of Woodrow Wilson, you might have some faint notion of what a human being should be to accept such compliments as deserved."[24]

But the honors came, and from many quarters. In 1913, Columbia University awarded him the honorary Doctor of Letters degree, "not only as an exponent of literature, but as an interpreter of national ideals [who] brought instruction and delight to two continents." Harvard awarded him the same degree in 1918, and the University of Strasburg granted the Doctor of Laws degree in 1920 for having "placed our country before his countrymen in a new light, and told them, in a well-known book, what they ought to think of the French family, and our *foyer*, of our universities and faculties."[25]

Wendell was from 1889 a fellow in the American Academy of Arts and Sciences, and from 1916 a fellow of the American Academy of Arts and Letters (whose memberships, of course, came to represent to the young writers in the 1920s the old grandfathers of American letters). In 1920, too, he was elected to the Board of Overseers of Harvard; and at his death the Sorbonne honored him by naming, for the first time, a lecture room after a foreigner.

A curious and ironic blend of growing success and growing pessimism marked the last years of the man who felt he had a genius for being profoundly, if honestly, in the wrong. Perhaps as a tribute to that honesty, and even as a recognition of his rightness too, came the large body of men to a surprise retirement dinner for Wendell in 1917. The guests, who presented the Charles Hopkinson portrait of Wendell to Harvard, composed an interesting cross section of the old and new literary culture: Bliss Perry, Brander Matthews, Charles Scribner, A. B. Lowell, Fred Robinson, George Lyman Kittredge, John Livingston Lowes, George P. Baker, Robert Herrick, John M. Manly, William Lyon Phelps, and Karl Young—all of whom, in spite of differences with Wendell, saw beneath the eccentric character who painted himself in that amber of irony to "the man in his intense genuineness, his real horror of affectation, the soundness of his independent thinking, the saneness of his first opinion, the generosity and magnitude of his heart."[26]

VIII *A Model of a Man*

We must, of course, distinguish the real Wendell from such tribute-dinner rhetoric, but Wendell's ambivalence, his double vision, make it difficult to describe him adequately. Santayana felt an equally mixed response to the colleague who displayed "tenderness and distinction of feeling," though with "no real distinction himself"; who presented "an interesting mixture of recklessness and propriety as an ideal character."[27] His daughter Edith remembered the gamut of her father's moods: he would range "from humor to irony, from sarcasm to pathos, from sunshine to storm, in such quick succession that one never knew what to expect; his mind grasped ideas wholesale and leapt forward with such rapidity that his bewildered audience was frequently left far behind, and one could never quite be sure what he really meant."[28]

The psychological awareness with which Wendell interpreted Hamlet's madness and his analysis of Jonathan Swift in a letter to

Kittredge on the "force of will" necessary to prevent social isolation from becoming mania seem to underline his self-analysis when referring to his potential for becoming a "chronic imaginary invalid": "I think I know my case and temperament well enough to regain self-control sometime, and escape this not comfortless state." In any case, he knew "if I stopped to ease myself, I should be done for."[29] Wendell's eccentricity was not uncalculated, and the picture that emerges of a man with a psychological need to compensate for deficiencies of which he was all too cognizant becomes even clearer in his identification with James Russell Lowell.

We discuss later Wendell's role in the critical tradition of Lowell and Norton, but Wendell's three commentaries on Lowell's life and work are important for what they tell us about the writer and not the subject; for, in James Russell Lowell, Wendell found an adequate ideal. He described Lowell as "a man of deep, but constantly various and whimsically incongruous, emotional nature, whose impulse to expression was hampered by all manner of importunate external impressions."[30] He was a "dozen men at once"; and Wendell's feeling that, when one knew Lowell, "his writing always seemed provokingly inadequate as an expression of his vitality" underlies our attention to Wendell's life as a necessary preface to his writing.

Wendell echoed the widespread appreciation for Lowell as "an incomparable teacher" when he wrote, "I think Lowell's course in Dante has meant more to me than any other of my college studies"—a view that a later generation of students expressed about Wendell's courses. The pattern of Wendell's own life reveals marked parallels to Lowell's. The younger Wendell who considered himself a mugwump and a potential Tammany man recalls the young reformist Lowell; and Lowell's late attention to political writing we see again in Wendell's later books on social and political theory. But, where Lowell was an active reformer before the war, Wendell only wanted to be one; and, where Lowell actually became a government diplomat, Wendell's political expression was always hidden behind the mask of a "mere man of letters." This contrast reveals the often-noted implications about a fading Boston culture in which Howells and Stedman were all too aware of their position in the apostolic succession of literary arbiters; but, while "the younger writers who would have enjoyed stepping into their [elders's] shoes were . . . , like Robert Grant and Barrett Wendell, a less authentic coinage of the Boston merit than their predecessors,"[31] the Boston of the 1890s found itself in the throes of a cultural inflation where not even the Lowell dollar could have purchased very much. Wendell, however, could identify with, and attempt to emulate, the Lowell force much easier than that of his business-world father.

In the qualities of geniality, wit, and learning, Wendell partook of the Lowell "ornaments" of a Tory mind, while in more particular aspects the parallels are startling: Wendell's daughter Mary remembered her father's shabby, loose clothing in nearly the same terms that Wendell used to describe Lowell's; both were "eccentric" in appearance. The quizzical, paradoxical Wendell whom we have met reflected Wendell's response to Lowell's "whimsical digressions." Wendell, who puzzled, startled, and shocked generations of Harvard students, wrote: "You never knew what he was going to say next . . . , in his own quizzical way—at one moment beautifully in earnest, at the next so whimsical that you could not quite make out what he meant—about whatever came into his head." Many former students recalled Wendell's uniqueness as a teacher; and, to Wendell, Lowell's methods were all his own. As a teacher, Wendell gave freely of himself and his ideas; and Wendell believed that Lowell "could teach us best by showing himself as he was."

The interpretation of the humanities that Wendell gained from Lowell as studies that kindle the imagination and thus the reason helps account for the views of Wendell's former students that he lectured the imagination as well as the intellect. Both critics defined literature as the enduring expression of the meaning of life, as man's ultimate record of human existence from previous ages; and our understanding of Wendell parallels Wendell's appreciation of Lowell's "honest, earnest work as a teacher, and not his spontaneous conduct as a human being." To Wendell, Lowell was not phony; and Wendell himself would exclaim, "God help me, I don't want to be a humbug!" Even their real fear in later life that all their teaching had been a waste, that they had thrown away more than they had gained, is also a significant parallel between the two.

Many problems are posed by these similarities, certainly not least among them the appreciation of a student for an effective teacher and the student's subsequent awareness of his own fears and responsibilities in that same Harvard tradition. But there is also the uncanny feeling that Wendell in describing Lowell described himself. When Wendell said Lowell "was really at his best when he let

himself be most fantastic, and this because of that whimsical instabil-
ity of temper, which he rarely managed quite to control"; or when
he said "somewhere about him there was always lurking a deep
seriousness strangely at odds with his obvious mannerisms, his occasional errors of taste, and his fantastic oddities of literary behavior,"
Wendell seemed to delineate not so much the figure Lowell was but
the man Wendell knew himself to be. Wendell clung increasingly to
the memory and tradition of Norton and Lowell as he aged, not
because of the insecurity caused by the changing time but because
of the insecurity that haunted his whole life.

IX *"Two Separate Lives"*

Wendell observed that "the most powerful minds reveal themselves in the trivialities of outward aspect," and H. L. Mencken
clearly felt this statement to be true of Wendell, though he saw the
answer to Wendell's "amazing contradictions and inconsistencies,
his endless flounderings between orthodoxy and heresy" to lie in the
"Viennese necromancer" Freud.[32] Van Wyck Brooks's famous high-
brow-lowbrow paradigm of the American mind fits Mencken's view
of Wendell's schizophrenia, for "always the sharply intelligent
Wendell hauled up and stayed romantic." Wendell's eccentricity,
the proof of his courage, illustrates Freud's analysis of jokes made at
one's own expense in order to sublimate those personal qualities
most hated and feared. The quality of weakness, of insecurity—
always opposed by his desire for verity—Wendell sought to control:
"Saturated with that pathos of distance, and being warm-hearted
and affectionate, he was intensely sentimental, yet heroically kept
his sentimentality in check and put up with things as they were.
That was his martyrdom."[33]

As Wendell noted of Lowell, "For all the self-consciousness inseparable from Yankee heritage, he was too wise to take himself too
seriously; for want of habitual valets, perhaps, he was no hero in his
own mind." Wendell, more aware of his weaknesses than his
strength, often is Prufrock, not Hamlet but an attendant lord, who
drew a cloak of protective irony about himself, the kind of irony, so
Wendell told Senator Lodge, that "results in an effect of opposition
to opponents rather than of serenely asserted principle." He drew
another telling distinction between himself and his friend William
James. The freedom, the optimism, the energy of James's intellect
works "like what I dream of Eden. As for me, my carriage, mental
and physical, sorrowfully reminds me of Adam's."[34]

This biographical sketch of Wendell raises a question difficult to answer, for juxtaposed to Wendell's physiological and psychological turning to paradox and the past is the fact that the social, political, and cultural chaos of the 1890s militated against his successful artistic or critical interaction with those times. The real question—perhaps unanswerable—is whether the pressure of a fading culture and of a turbulent era led Wendell to the characteristics we have described or whether Wendell's personal problems only heightened and compounded the inevitable debilitation of a man caught in the midst of wholesale cultural transition. The sense of futility felt by Wendell and others is real enough in his life and work; its causes are less clear. In any case, his heredity and environment worked against him; he was perhaps too much of a conservative and too much influenced by the Lowell family tree to be the real rebel and discoverer that his intelligence might otherwise have led him to be. The armchair reformist zeal of transcendentalist Boston could hardly work in "a world awry," and, because 35 percent of Boston's population was foreign by 1900, the former security that had isolated the older Brahmins had disappeared. While that Boston still played a vital role in the history of art and ideas in America, Wendell always remembered that Charles Norton had once described the saddest historical figure as the Roman citizen of culture faithful to his ideals in the third or fourth century. Wendell felt he shared that fate.

The tragedy of Wendell's life is that, as a product of his time, he lacked the initiative, the energy, and the courage to alter that time; and he knew it. He described his ever-present mood as one in which he felt too old for change but saw change surging everywhere. While we may question whether Wendell would have felt at home even in the best of times, it is evident that he was always too old, forever out of his time; as Thomas Beer says, he was "rather an emblem than a man."[35] And the end of the nineteenth century was not the best of times; it was an age of sharp antithesis, like most; but it was more traumatic in terms of cultural and national integrity.

We must be cautious when generalizing about periods of transition. Writers in every age somehow feel themselves contemporary with momentous change, and most major literary figures could be cited as exemplary of some transitional development. Today men know rapid change as integral to modern life, but the men who watched the approaching twentieth century knew stability far more intimately. Time and time again Wendell declared, "I hate change." The rapidity of change in all areas of late nineteenth-century life must have been frightening to Wendell and his contemporaries. Santayana's diagnosis of the split between American will and American intellect seems like an understatement, but the effect of this opposition clearly meant enervation. The Mark Twain who hovered between Boston and the western frontier illustrates the frustration of a divided and confused mentality. Like Matthew Arnold's figure in "Stanzas from the Grande Chartreuse," Barrett Wendell and his friends were caught between a dying world and an unborn one; without faith to turn confidently to the old, without power to enfranchise the new, they hesitated, torn between the old "unity" and a "new" multiplicity, between classical authority and modern iconoclasm. We sense often that part of the defeatism in Wendell and Adams lies not in what they disliked of the new so much as in their awareness of belonging to the old. William Dean Howells felt the 1912 dinner in his honor was all wrong; it was out of joint with the time, and no one knew it. And Brooks Adams wrote his brother Henry in 1896: "It is time we perished. The world is tired of us." Henry Adams expressed his own feeling of isolation to Wendell: "We roll on the ground and sprinkle dust on our heads in consciousness of our miserable state, but we can get no help. The disease has reached a point where we are obligated to compose our music for ourselves alone, and of course this sort of composition means that we go on repeating our faults. No echo whatever comes back."[36] In Wendell's case, as we shall see, there were many echoes; for, though not wholly confident about the future, he did not shout into a box canyon.

Once more we may describe Wendell by Lowell's light; as Fred Lewis Pattee said of Wendell's old teacher, his "influence was greater than his writings. He was a Janus figure caught midway between two generations and standing comfortably with neither."[37] This is even truer of Wendell, caught between the world of James R. Lowell and Amy Lowell. Santayana felt that "something admirable was wasted in him. The age made it impossible for him to do well what he would have loved to do."[38] At the same time, no writer, artist, or critic can create against the back pressure of his emotions and that pressure in Wendell comprised physical and emotional weakness, professional uncertainty and insecurity, and temperamental aversion to change.

By reason of his birthdate, Wendell's career fell between the two major creative periods in American literature. The major names of his youth represented the first American renaissance and those of his old age the second; for *Leaves of Grass* appeared in Wendell's first year; and T. S. Eliot's *Poems*, Sinclair Lewis's *Main Street*, and Eugene O'Neill's *Anna Christie* appeared in his last. The sixty years between those dates were full of energy, experiment, failure, uncertainty, and hope as America once more came of age. Few great literary names emerged significantly from the social, political, economic, and cultural flux of those years. Writers like Mark Twain, Henry James, Emily Dickinson, Theodore Dreiser are major. The crowd below them, from John W. DeForest to Winston Churchill, rarely managed to encounter their age or to control their form to create first-rate work, and Barrett Wendell falls into this latter class as one of the more typical products of his time. He wrote to Sir Robert White-Thomson in 1908: "We are passed into an ethnologic era as new as that of fire, of the wheel, of metal. Not inconceivably, the trouble men of your time feel, and of mine, is only that we must confront the new era with the ideas of the old. But it needs strong faith to feel buoyant."[39] The exigencies of the age, of his profession, of his personality coalesced to thwart any consistent creativity in Wendell and because of his eccentricity, his Tory prejudices, his antiquarian concern for the past, Wendell was swept under a large rug regarded as the late nineteenth-century failure in criticism.

CHAPTER 2

The Puritan Priest

IT is hardly difficult to understand Wendell's remarkable sympathy for Cotton Mather. He wrote to his friend William James in 1900: "I love the memory of Cotton Mather; and should be happier in a world that hadn't been graced by Channing or Emerson."[1] In many ways Cotton Mather symbolized for Wendell an age of religious certainty that had eroded since the 1840s in Boston to a period of "devout free thought." Moreover, if James Russell Lowell provides us with clues to Wendell's psychological state, Mather reveals a very strong parallel to Wendell as another example of a man born after his time and forced to live in a world he could face only with utmost courage. Alan Heimert describes the troubled soul of Wendell's Mather as "curiously typical" of so "fragmenting a culture as that of provincial New England . . . this melancholy country— divided against itself, abandoning its heritage yet seeking to give the ancestral faith new meaning."[2]

The story of Cotton Mather's futile and singular attempt to re-gather the threads of his father's faith also strikingly parallels Wendell's thwarted efforts to achieve the success worthy of his father's trust. Yet again there is irony, for Mather had faith in the Calvinist creed to sustain him; Wendell had only his defensive wit: Old New England possessed absolute certainty about who the devil was, he maintained, but his New England had no certainty about what the devil anything was. Nonetheless, *Cotton Mather*, the first scholarly book of this ironic, defensive, whimsical Wendell was positive; it challenged popular views held in late nineteenth-century Cambridge, and it still stands as one of his best books.[3]

By the end of the nineteenth century, the harshness of Puritan dogma had evaporated into the now infamous Victorian morality; its squeamishness, its sexual timidity, its high moral tone, and its inability to call a spade a spade—reflected in book banning and in

44

temperance movements—came under severe indictment by writers in the twentieth century. In a rough and tumble modern America, art needed vigorously to confront life, not in its idealistic or even sweetly realistic moods, but frankly and honestly, seeing its depths as well as its heights, its ugliness and corruption as well as its beauty. To defend Cotton Mather, at the wellspring of the unrealistic if not hypocritical faith, was heresy.

It was, therefore, no simple matter, even in the 1890s to write a sympathetic analysis of Cotton Mather. The Unitarian and transcendental movements had some years previously moved Harvard solidly into the liberal camp and Mather's superstitious barbarism made him one of its least admired ancestors, an attitude only strengthened by Moses Coit Tyler's negative assessment of the early Puritan. Wendell's *Mather* caused considerable consternation at Harvard in 1891, though contemporary reviews praised the study as a faithful interpretation. It appeared in the Makers of America series and was later called by Wendell's former student and colleague Kenneth Murdock the "best biography" of Mather and "one of the great American biographies." And Heimert has called it still "the best single-volume study" of the "Puritan Priest."[4]

H. L. Mencken's claim that Wendell "clung to the superstition that the preposterous theologians of [New England's] early days constituted an intellectual aristocracy, and even wrote a book eulogizing the most absurd of them," illustrates rather nicely the early twentieth-century tendency to misread the immediate past because of widespread anti-Puritan bias. V. L. Parrington found much to criticize in the "gentle light of filial loyalty" cast over the Puritans by Harvard historians, but he could still praise Wendell's assessment of Cotton Mather's *Magnalia:* "The purpose of the book has nowhere been better stated than by Professor Wendell."[5]

I *Mather's Own Voice*

Wendell in *Cotton Mather* pursues chronologically the life and career of the eighteenth-century theocrat with a brief commentary on Mather's spiritual inheritance as well as on the cultural and historical context of his day. And, because Wendell feels that Mather can be accepted as a "singularly veracious historian of himself," he allows Mather to speak for himself from the pages of his published work, his notebooks, and his diaries. *The Critic* review summarized Wendell's study as revealing Mather "not alone as his-

tory thus far has shown him: not merely, on one side as the most
loquacious pedant, yet in truth most learned scholar, of his time; not
merely as the egotist, the mystic, the theocrat, the promoter of the
Salem trials; not yet merely as the author of that unique, quaintly
inclusive, survey of his compeers . . . ; but he has set before us a
man who may in justice be absolved from the charge of obstinate
bad faith and concealed recognition of terrible mistakes."[6]

Wendell holds no brief to defend Cotton Mather, though later
generations were to accuse him of this; rather, says Wendell, "my
object is to tell what manner of man he was, what manner of world
he lived in, why—with all his oddities and failings that are to us so
grotesque—he seems well worth remembering" (3). Wendell's
method, characteristic of his general ambivalence, was to obscure
himself as much as possible in order to let Mather himself speak
through his personal diaries. Wendell's objective in using Mather's
diaries is made clear in his statement that, "before we can judge him
aright, we must strive to see him as he saw himself" (224). Wendell's
method leads him to attend rather to Mather's interior life than his
external, to give rather sketchy views of the historical figure, and to
accept the often inaccurate historical data provided by earlier biog-
raphers and historians. He tends to attribute to Mather's day the
continued intellectual vigor of Puritanism that was more characteristic of John Cotton's day, and at times he prefigures his own disen-
chantment with American society, his own reactionary tendencies
by his attention to the "desertion" of Mather in the 1690s by the
very people he so diligently strove to serve (106–10). Wendell also
refuses to question whether Mather acted tyrannically to control the
will of his congregation or pastorally to liberate their spirit, nor does
he recognize Mather's intensification of his personal experience in
diaries that he meant to be an inspirational legacy for his children.

But the thesis of Wendell's study of Mather—that "he never
ceased striving, amid endless stumblings and errors, to do his duty"
(224) and to strive sincerely to discover his life in God's will—emerges
from a very nicely achieved balance in characterization. If Wendell
does not step overtly into his work to criticize Mather, he nonetheless allows the Puritan's own words to judge him. This balance, or
paradox according to *The Critic* review, depicts "unfaltering credulity" which begins to appear "almost like heroism." Lindsay Swift
wrote that Wendell "with a somewhat lavish gesture, has thrown a
mantle of charity over Mather, and yet he has so disposed it as to

reveal his nakedness and weakness."[7] What Wendell achieves through careful presentation of diary passages is a remarkable penetration into the inner mind of Mather—a delineation which, if not one of depth psychology, at least subtly reveals the intensity of Mather's personal struggle with faith, with the important father-son partnership, with his soul-searching attention to pastoral and civic endeavors, with his fears and motivations during the witchcraft trials, and with the self-delusion and subsequent errors in Mather's will to power.

Wendell's attitude toward witchcraft in *Cotton Mather* is illustrative. As *The Critic* reviewer noted, Wendell was the "first of historical writers to take the view that the witchcraft declarations are not to be repelled altogether as born of malice or delusion." The vogue of Spiritualism, Christian Science, and Madame Blavatsky; the widespread fascination in Wendell's Boston with extrasensory phenomena; and his own personal experience with "psychic research" prior to writing *Mather* influenced him so much that, when studying Mather's diaries, Wendell encountered a startling "familiarity" with the evidence of the witch trials—the evidence not of delusion but of real evil, the presence of something primordial, dark, "unholy," "demoralizing" (68–71). For Mather, for Hawthorne, and for the young Hawthornesque author of the *Duchess Emilia*, the power of blackness was real and not to be ignored; for Wendell occult phenomena, seances, automatic writing, and the like revealed not positive but unhealthy depths in man. Therefore, the example of Salem proves not the blind superstition of Mather but the strength of his spiritual perceptivity as to the reality of those dark forces in man.

While Wendell agrees with Mather's belief that such forces should be conquered, he notes that Mather's vanity—his conviction that he seriously spoke for the Lord in the trials—"established a monument to human frailty" (72–74). Wendell writes, "I have said enough, I think, to show why I heartily sympathize with those who in 1692 did their utmost to suppress [witchcraft]; to show, too, why the fatally tragic phase of the witch trials seems to me, not the fact that there was no crime to condemn, but the fact that the evidence on which certain wretched people were executed proves, on scrutiny, utterly insufficient" (71). Wendell believes that posterity, in its condemnation of Mather, has confused belief in witchcraft with insistence on the validity of spectral evidence. Mather held the first but also admitted to "a growing doubt as to how far so mysterious and terrible an evil can be dealt with by so material an engine as the criminal law" (78). Though Mather never admitted wrongdoing, his diaries reveal constant doubt over his crucial role in the witch trials. Perhaps because of the doubt and the reactions against the trials afterward, Mather displayed a weakening of nerve and far less public enthusiasm. Wendell's enthusiasm, too, is tempered by his realization that the witches who succumbed to the power of evil were far less to blame than the tyrannous, pious majority who persecuted them. And Mather's role in the witch trials, where sixteenth-century religion encountered eighteenth-century rationality and "broke the power of theocracy," left him a life "of constant, crescent failure" (65).

II *"Passionate Idealism"*

Wendell's underlying attitude toward Mather is one he expounds again and again in *Stelligeri*, the *Literary History*, and the later political works. Part of Wendell's bias toward the academic world of his day was the increasing emphasis on Germanic scholarship, which meant to Wendell the seeking after sterile facts and missing the larger meanings. His motivation in *Cotton Mather* led not to political or economic considerations but to the understanding of "subjective matters," of the "fervent spirit," of the "passionate enthusiasm of the Puritans." He said that the "somewhat grotesque austerity of their consequent aspect and manners has combined with the rather lifeless formalism of Yankee Puritanism in its decline to obscure the truth that early Calvinism was an intensely ideal, imaginative faith."[8]

Even though Wendell decried in his own day the loss of a religious and social order characteristic of eighteenth-century life, he hardly approved the moral fastidiousness and literary euphemism of late nineteenth-century "Puritanism." He was no Puritan; he urged no return to Calvinist dogma. "I am more Calvinist every year," he wrote William James, "except in the points where Calvinism quarrels with Rome."[9] His wit may be defensive here, but it indicates a personal distance from the old Protestant creeds. His appreciation for Puritanism was cultural. Just as Catholicism was valued by Wendell's former professor, the medieval scholar Charles Eliot Norton, for the unity it gave life in the Middle Ages, Puritanism provided that same social order for the seventeenth and early eighteenth centuries in the New England of America.

Furthermore, Wendell as a historian saw great meaning in that old faith for analyzing the nature of the American mind. It was no attempt to escape contemporary adherence to the environmental emphasis of Charles Darwin and Hippolyte Taine that led Wendell to assert the preeminence in Puritan thought of life with God in the hereafter rather than of life on earth now. Indeed, Wendell's literary histories, as well as his political writings, reveal both environmental and evolutionary principles as he traces the progression of American ideals. Wendell read the intense Puritan imagination and ideality, amid a world of social pressure far less tense and black than in Europe, as the solution to the puzzle as to "how so profoundly fatalistic a creed could possibly prove a motive power strong enough to result not only in individual lives but in a corporate life, that was destined to grow into a national life, of passionate enthusiasm, and of abnormal moral as well as material activity."[10]

Ideality to Wendell meant inner vitality—the impetus from things unseen; and he finds that force in the Puritan doctrine of election, the effort on the part of the Puritan fathers to assert their will in conjunction with God (6, 22). That effort, the "emotional enthusiasm constantly stimulated by the unrecognized impulse of selfish human curiosity," gave rise to the intensive Puritan imagination which in turn burned itself out. Wendell points to the *Magnalia* as one of the major documents of the seventeenth century for its lucidity, its "veracity of spirit," its insights into the Puritan ideal (118). While he is not correct in considering Mather as Puritanism's "last, its most typical" incarnation, he recognizes not only the powerful Puritan imagination, its metaphoric modes of expression in the *Magnalia*, but also its backward-looking attempt to preserve old values. Wendell's insight into the profundity of Puritan spirituality, the intense emotional reality of its intercourse with demons and angels, its awareness of spiritual lessons in the natural world, and its errors and solitary qualities led Wendell to an early appreciation of William James's *Varieties of Religious Experience*, but he also affirms the influence of environment on this spiritual fervor: "In no serious study of corporate character can the serious student for a moment forget . . . the crushing, distorting influence of those petty material facts to which we give the convenient name of every-day life";[11] and, if Wendell too easily accepts the spiritual, imaginative energy of the Puritans as maintaining its vitality so late as Cotton Mather's day, he nonetheless sees the eternal appearance of "grim,

untruthful formalism" in Mather (224). Still, the ideality underlying
the hope of being one of God's elect and the spiritual, imaginative
enthusiasm of the Puritan faith coalesce to form part of the intense
ideality that Wendell thinks characterizes the American innocence,
its "national inexperience."

In a new world, where all the old social forces and pressures of
European society were replaced by a concern to build a new society
wherein "the will of man is made perfectly and immutably free to
good alone in the state of glory only" (18), Puritanism, especially in
the life of Cotton Mather, posed a major contradiction between
"theocracy and democracy, priesthood and protestantism" (19); and
it became in Wendell's life Brahminism and democracy. In Mather's
lifetime, the power of democracy, the force of individualism, and
the standard of material success as a measure of election were
dramatically breaking the chains of theocracy. But the tension, the
paradox, and the dilemma posed by these alternatives in Mather's
life were those same tensions that Wendell felt between the authority of a New England aristocracy and the energy of the American
common man. Mather's diaries are opened to show the man whose
emotions came either from God or Satan, never from less exalted
sources. Mather and his father stand out as heroic figures whose
faith sustained them in their struggles with the crown, with royal
governors, with the needs of their parish, with the tribulations of
their families, and with the demands of their bodies. Perhaps the
significance of Cotton Mather for Barrett Wendell lay in the
maintenance, if not the resolution, of these tensions.

The death of Mather's father Increase is ominous for Wendell, for
the older Mather represented the last generation of undoubting
faith: "Whoever has followed the history of Harvard College,
through Unitarianism, to that more shadowy heresy still which calls
itself unsectarian religion,—even though he rejoice, as I do, in the
unfettered spiritual freedom of the greatest stronghold of American
Protestantism,—must know that the grim old man read the future
right. If the faith from which he never swerved be true, then as-
suredly we of the later times are lost" (212). Wendell reveals to us
the Cotton Mather who lost his father, his wives, eleven of his
fourteen children, even the support of his churches, but never his
faith. His doubts, however, led defensively to more vigorous, more
tyrannous assertions of that faith. Students who described Wendell
as an actor echoed Wendell's description of Mather's "histrionic

insincerity," the mark of an isolated priest who clung in the face of change to outworn tradition.

There is a dilemma in Wendell's *Mather;* and it derives from the paradox of a man "veracious while inaccurate, honest if prejudiced, devout though narrow, energetic and laborious while lacking sound sense and judgment,"[12]—the paradox of a man Wendell calls "self-seeking, vain, arrogant, inconsistent, mischievous," yet sincerely a man of duty (223–24). As Wendell balances the external tyrant and bigot with the internal man of devout conviction, his method allows him to manage the paradox; but Wendell wants to emphasize not the man who failed to realize "that Protestantism can have no priesthood," but the figure who stands as the fountainhead of "devout free thought," the contrast between the Puritan sense of a divinely elected hierarchy and the English common-law tradition of equality.

III *In Memoriam*

Wendell's *Cotton Mather* is the work of a literary mugwump, the young "blind democrat" and Cleveland supporter, who attempts to show in Cotton Mather not just a New England tradition of order but of idealistic freedom. The book is a contribution by Wendell to the "effort to reinvigorate New England which found ultimate expression in 'The Will to Believe.' "[13] Because of Mather's devotion and his faith in democratic Protestant equality, Wendell tends to denigrate Mather's errors. Wendell's optimism, though, like Mather's faith, gave way ultimately to a conservative fear that democracy finally is a sworn foe of excellence.

At the end of his study, then, Mather emerges as a representative of the devout free thought of Puritanism's faith in the priesthood of the believer; of the idealistic fervor which the doctrine of election imparted to daily life; of the error and tyranny resulting from excessive zeal and enthusiasm; and, in the witch trials, of the tyranny of the majority over a minority despite that majority's zealous sense of right. Between 1892, when Wendell described himself as a sincere democrat, and 1893, when he despaired at a world with which he felt inadequate to compete, we see him withdrawing from his democratic enthusiasms because of the excesses and failures of reform movements in the 1880s, just as Mather had withdrawn from his public demonstration of religious emotion after his self-doubts over the witch trials. It is easy to understand Wendell's love for the

memory of Cotton Mather, for the youthful Wendell resurrected
the memory of a man of sincere duty; and the older Wendell asserted that, while he found in Mather's faith or practice little he
"could literally or actually share," there was "in the strength of his
conservative enthusiasm something which commanded my heartfelt
sympathy."[14] What sparked Wendell's move toward conservatism in
the 1890s is perhaps impossible to discover; but in 1894 he still
could posit Mather's "passionate eagerness to preserve unaltered
what the Puritans believed to be their divinely sanctioned system of
faith and government" against the narrowness, pettiness, tyranny,
and absurdities of the Puritans.

As Wendell saw the values of a changing world replacing those of
old Boston, as he saw a threat to liberty in the mob, he revered the
integrity of the minister who—despite societal disillusionment with
his faith, his personal errors, his misguided leadership ability—
could still struggle to do his duty. If indeed the 1890s marked Wendell's own loss of nerve, the loss was not total. The personalities of
both Mather and Wendell appeared bathed in the light of paradox;
enthusiasm and error, election and equality, free thought and divine
grace must operate together in delicate tension. Enthusiasm con-
trasted with human depravity led less, perhaps, to inaction than to
that ironic ambivalence in Wendell, who (though no Puritan) revered the influence of Puritanism, who (no equalitarian) appreciated
its belief in individual priesthood, who (no optimist) applauded the
sanguine Puritan imaginative energy.

Cotton Mather remains a good study of the Puritan priest and
provides a suggestive metaphor as well for Wendell's own career:
"Pure in motive, noble in purpose, his whole life was one unending
effort to strengthen in himself that phase of human nature whose
inner token is a riot of mystical emotion, whose outward signs are
unwitting manifestations of unfettered credulity and unmeant
fraud" (226).

CHAPTER 3

The Ideals of America

W HILE Wendell's initial work probed the historical-cultural matrix of American literature, the bulk of his writing after 1905 dealt with American political and social rather than literary theory. The reviewer of *Liberty, Union, and Democracy* (1906) in *Putnam's* felt that Wendell's "clarity suggests that the philosophy of history, rather than literature, is Professor Wendell's real field";[1] and William MacDonald in *The Nation* remarked that Wendell's "study of American literature has led him to a juster appreciation of the political ideas which, in moulding the American character, have made American literature possible."[2] To perceive more clearly, then, Wendell's literary theories, we need to look first at his conception of the ideals underlying American literature.

By 1900, the reformist concerns of the Genteel Tradition had—under the pressures of industrialization, urbanization, and immigration—become largely antidemocratic and reactionary. In the twentieth century, it has become fashionable to link Barrett Wendell with genteel writers in part because of their shared pessimism. Yet this sense of skepticism toward contemporary life, a feeling of alienation and despair toward American society, was no less characteristic of earlier periods in American thought than it was of Wendell's day and even of the 1920s and 1930s. Moreover, we may associate Wendell far more easily with other famous pessimists in the universities than with the editors of mass magazines concerned to dictate standards of taste to the vast middle-class public. Henry and Brooks Adams, William Graham Sumner, Thorstein Veblen, George Santayana, and Josiah Royce all shared a negative vision toward the pious, optimistic buoyance of the time. Wendell was perhaps not so tough-minded as these famous contemporaries, but he, like them, sought to assert a system of value that was at once reactionary and positive. As early as 1895, Wendell described his growing disillusionment with the country, feeling that "Democracy, in old world or new, seems little better than a caricature of government": its power promotes "tyranny, dishonesty, petty baseness, corruption" in its leaders, and the "better classes" eschew it altogether.[3] Yet his reputation in those years rested on his promotion of English composition and American literature.

Not until the publication of *Liberty, Union, and Democracy* (1906), *The Privileged Classes* (1908), and *The Mystery of Education* (1909) did Wendell's reputation acquire the tenor of notoriety. His *Privileged Classes* created an uproar among the working men and newspapers of Chicago and Boston, and the *New York Times* described him as "low in his mind" over the nation's political health. A *Putnam* review pictured him somewhat misanthropically "clouded with doubt"; and *Scribner's*, because of the poor sales of these books, was forced to reject his social-political articles as disastrously unpopular. The implicit optimism of *English Composition*, of the *Literary History*, and of the Sorbonne Lectures gave way to an increasing despair. Yet, as late as 1917, he urged not just visions of an Anglo-Saxon imperialism, which he shared with his friend Senator Lodge, but hopes for a democratic world government "by common consent": "In such an empire the common authority of all would protect the independence of each part, enforcing the law of peace, sparing those who submit to it, checking oppression, suppressing rebellion. All this such common authority must do not in a name foreign to any, but in a name common to every part—for such common authority must be based on the humble and devoted consent of all."[4]

I *Democratic Origins*

Of Wendell's books on social and political matters, *Liberty, Union, and Democracy* (1906) expresses most systematically ideas that may be found as early as *Stelligeri* (1893) and which underlie significantly his thesis in the *Literary History*. The fact that the book of 1906 grew out of ideas that we discover in Wendell's class lectures and especially in his lectures at the Sorbonne and the Lowell Institute probably accounts for much of the rigor of its system, whose thesis, as he follows the development of the three concepts in its title, is simply that "the native character of America is marked and unbroken from the foundation of colonies in Virginia and New England." His approach is to consider "the manner in which America has conceived and has responded to the political ideals most conscious and most potent during one hundred and thirty years of our national history."[5] The book remains important for us not only because of its delineation of Wendell's theory about American ideals but for its revelation of Wendell's own idealism.

His views are not incompatible with the idea of America as the New Garden and the pioneer as the New Adam who was motivated by a consuming ideal and convinced of his ability to establish a new order, to build the City on the Hill. Wendell diverges, however, from more liberal or Jeffersonian concepts of the New World man, the yeoman as the source of national strength; he looks back at the sources of early American idealism to document his faith not only in equality but in excellence. What motivated early settlers of America, Wendell maintains, was the prerevolutionary spirit of seventeenth-century Englishmen, a spirit of idealism; for such men, upset over the current state of affairs, were seeking a new "Golden Age, whether a lost one or one not yet attained by human error" (38). Englishmen suffered through revolution and civil war in 1642, but the colonial prerevolutionaries—Roundheads in New England; Cavaliers in Virginia—missed the revolution and spent their energy in developing the American colonies. England passed through its Puritan era, its Restoration, and settled into eighteenth-century neoclassicism; but America continued to maintain the more revolutionary ideals of the early seventeenth century—individual liberty and the possibility of success through merit. A difference still remains, asserts Wendell, between a "radical America and conservative England"; in America, "the things of the spirit are still apt to seem more inwardly true; to be more potent" (42).

Wendell's theories are representative of the conservative tradition attacked by such historians of the 1920s as V. L. Parrington who quotes negatively Wendell's statement that "the innumerable thoughtless assertions of human equality . . . if duly reasoned out by forces of ordinary logic, would start us headlong toward anarchy" (64). Yet we cannot deny the fact of ideas like Wendell's in our national culture. The New Humanism, most eloquently articulated by Irving Babbitt and Paul Elmer More, carried Wendell's kind of conservatism further into the twentieth century by pointing out that democracy degenerates into anarchy and tyranny if the voice of the majority replaces the wisdom of genuine leaders. The drive for democratic equality has always been tempered by more or less aris-

tocratic concepts of leadership and creativity; indeed, as the
economic interpreters of the Constitution point out, the very formal
basis of our government is a function of conservative, property-
oriented interests. Even the more traditional view holds the Constitution to be a compromise between an egalitarian Jeffersonian
tradition and an aristocratic Hamiltonian one.

The Puritan heritage, in the development of American political
and cultural thought, is a complex matter; but it absorbed much of
Wendell's attention despite the fact that he felt serious antipathy
toward the Puritanical prudery of his own day. His sympathetic
reading of Cotton Mather attributes an increased sensitivity, if not
to Calvinist orthodoxy, to the idealistic fervor of Calvinism. He feels
that the theological idealism "enforced, strengthened, and defined
among our forefathers the more general idealism which pervaded all
pre-revolutionary Englishmen" (59). Theologically, election de-
creed some men "nobler and better than other men"; so therefore,
while he recognizes that the theological impulse was "not democratic in origin" (70), Wendell finds in the coalescence of both political
and religious dissent an impulse and a structure, albeit simplified,
for the kind of idealism he asserts in 1906. Writing about political
freedom and divine election, he states that, "clearly enough, this
principle was bound to develop into such democratic ones as Americans now generally cherish" (70). Surely Andrew Carnegie at least
cherished it as part of his Gospel of Wealth, but so did Irving
Babbitt in his search for the good life.

The test of excellence by merit became the problem inherent in
the secularization of the American Dream, and Wendell was quite
aware of that problem: the right, the freedom to make a success in
the world, may be motivated by a kind of idealism; but, since *material* success became the sign early of God's favor with his elect and
later the sign of the individual's own ability, "actual life may appear
at odds with this idealism" (72). Practical considerations, as well as
religious motivations, conditioned this split with actual life on the
frontier. Once again, the argument over the cultural pressure from
the East, as opposed to the frontier thesis of American thought, has
so polarized our thinking that we cast Wendell purely on the side of
an effete, conservative aristocracy; but he notes explicitly that pre-
revolutionary idealism and spiritual idealism imported from the Old
World were modified by the need of settlers "to make a wilderness
habitable and to establish among themselves a practical system of

government," with the inevitable conflict or confluence of ideality and pragmatism. No wonder then, Wendell says, "that strangers who have observed our outward semblance . . . should suppose us at heart material and practical" (73). He sounds much like Walt Whitman, Hamilton Wright Mabie, and the genteel critics in expressing a democratic spirituality underlying and motivating its materiality.

Prerevolutionary idealism, Calvinist theology, and the frontier wilderness, then, formed in the seventeenth and eighteenth centuries an important amalgam of the love of liberty and deference to authority, a tradition which acquired not a beginning but a definition with the Declaration of Independence, the first real assertion that this new people *had come* into existence. As denoting the birth of our national consciousness, it is important because America, "unnoticed and unnoticing, developed between 1620 and 1775 a new historical continuity"—a new native tradition of its own "in isolation from Europe and thus apart from the pressing and incessant checks of traditional historical continuity" (80–81). Wendell's theory of the American Revolution was well known, and even attacked in his own day, but it was not new. Tocqueville had earlier maintained that Americans achieved a state of democracy without having to undergo a democratic revolution, that Americans were born free without having to become free.

In terms of the radical upheavals of the French Revolution, Wendell maintains in Burkeian terms that the American revolution was conservative: "to maintain against reactionary innovation that historical continuity, those immemorial traditions of our own, which the unbroken experience of five generations had proved favorable among ourselves to prosperity and righteousness. Alone of revolutions ours was essentially conservative" (86).

Van Wyck Brooks, as a major spokesman for the twentieth century revolt against Wendell's generation, found Wendell "paradoxical" in his defense of American traditions because he missed the significance of all the revolution stood for; therefore, Wendell "missed the meaning of his country." Part of Brooks's concern evolved from his liberal reevaluation of the American tradition, but he also misread Wendell's interpretation as deploring the revolution because it "had sundered us from England and the guidance of the British ruling class."[6] Such a view once again involves the erroneous conception of Wendell as simply a Tory anglophile—the same conception that caused many twentieth-century critics to misinterpret his negative pronouncements on American literature as a function of his biased appreciation of English literature.

By the end of the nineteenth century, for Wendell, the American form of government and its bible the Constitution had attained religious authority throughout the country. American imperialism and manifest destiny were as divinely sanctioned, because of the universal rightness of the Constitution, as were the early Puritan efforts to establish a theocracy in the new promised land. Wendell's concerns, like John Fiske's in his influential *Civil Government in the United States with Some Reference to its Origins* (1890), are to show the roots of that government in English tradition. Wendell argues that our literature and our revolution served merely to reiterate not only the new world tradition but also a tradition of English rights and liberties as old as the Magna Carta. We discover an idealistic seriousness in Wendell's words about the revolution: "its ultimate work was hardly destructive at all; it preserved, rather, it sustained, and it strengthened the character, the ideals, the rights, the aspirations of a nation which the tremendous course of history has already made the oldest in the world."[7]

II *Liberty*

Wendell's views were hardly out of step with the widespread Teutonic racism and imperialism at the end of the nineteenth century which closed its eyes to growing disenfranchisement of the Negro in the South; expressed unhappiness over Irish, Jewish, and Italian immigration; and supported American colonization of Cuba, Puerto Rico, and the Philippines. Moreover, it is important to understand Wendell's idealistic though conservative theory, at once pro-American and aware of a real American tradition, in order to aid our understanding later of his thesis of "national inexperience" in the *Literary History*. His *Liberty, Union, and Democracy* might well have been titled *A Political History of America*, since, as in the *Literary History*, his concern lies in the ideals motivating American expression. The first of these ideals is liberty, a concept held very differently by the North and the South. In New England, because of social and economic forces (which though unspecified by Wendell we may easily understand to be things like national protective tariffs and interstate commerce regulation for Yankee industry), the governmental unit came increasingly to be the United States rather than the individual state. Subsequent emphases on *personal* liberty grew from a stronger concern for freedom from privilege and established authority protected by the ballot, trial by jury, and habeas corpus. In the South, however, social distinctions put greater emphasis on *local* liberty, a function of the rigid plantation system wherein the owner was also the political leader, and the poor whites, like the slaves, lacked any real voice (142–44).

Wendell succinctly says that, "when the social and economic conditions of any region remain so comparatively stable that generation after generation preserves the same broad traits of character, it is pretty safe to conclude its general conceptions of political ideals will not alter much" (150). The question of slavery, says Wendell, was originally not so much a moral problem as an economic one. In the industrially diversifying North, free labor came to be far more profitable; but, in the South, slaves were not only profitable to a one-crop economy but increasingly necessary; and, by 1860, slavery was viewed as almost divinely sanctioned. In the North, on the other hand, slavery was unnecessary, and it came to be illegal and was felt to be immoral by 1860 (153–55). Wendell's analysis of the political ideal of liberty, very interestingly, if largely implicitly, rests on sociological and economic insights long before that approach was seriously used by historians as a scientific instrument.

III *Union*

For Wendell, then, the Civil War represents an honest conflict of Northern and Southern ideals, ones widely divergent as a result of their incompatible economic systems. By 1860, union became a concept for the North that was coequal in importance with liberty; but Daniel Webster's idea of liberty and union "now and forever, one and inseparable" was in radical conflict with John C. Calhoun's and Southerners' insistence that the United States was not a nation but a union that could be dissolved. Both views logically derived from the different ideals in the North about personal liberty and in the South about local liberty, and both concepts got support from religious and philosophical values, especially in New England where both individualism and unity were celebrated in the "untrammelled outburst of devout free thought whose lasting exponent is Emerson" (23). While transcendentalism was developing from the roots of English law and Calvinistic theology, a conspiracy of silence spread throughout the South about the conditions of slavery. The integrity of all these facts is important, for in reality Wendell concerns himself here not merely with political ideas but with social, economic, and religious facts—forces inherent in the national ideals of America.

IV Democracy

The last concept in Wendell's troika of ideals is democracy. The revolution asserted American liberty, the Civil War affirmed national union, but the subsequent emphasis on democracy, on the average man with average talent, and a majority vote seriously disturbed Wendell. The blind worship of equality threatened the traditional values of excellence and property and thus the very strength of America. The liberal *Nation* positively assessed Wendell's point of view: He is not the first to show the tyranny of the majority, and the grave possibilities of social order as demanded by unions. "It is rather the deft and cultured way in which he pricks the bubble of our conceit and complacency that makes his writing interesting. Persons of socialistic bent will not relish being told that the real American Revolution is not the war that separated us from Great Britain, but the social change which has lead large segments of society to view with equanimity socialistic schemes for the expropriation of private property."[8]

Wendell's adherence is to the English strain of democratic theory as opposed to more radical French concepts of equality. Like the New Humanists later, Wendell regarded Jean-Jacques Rousseau as an enemy and not as a hero of democratic theory. The tyrannical creed of equality—of social leveling, "shackling ability, decrying excellence and asserting privilege for the irresponsible"—is a threat to one of the oldest ideals of order, of natural distinctions in American history, the distinction which early derived in New England from the doctrine of election, which first the clergy and then the other professions in this country made manifest. That this view sounds like that of the famous last Brahmin is certainly clear—even more so when Wendell recites Oliver Wendell Holmes's famous celebration of the Brahmin "untitled aristocracy" in New England.

Horace Traubel's review of Wendell's book characterized the more radical view toward these issues: "The old ideal of liberty only prepared the way for political freedom. . . . The new ideal prepares the way for economic freedom. Wendell criticizes the Declaration because it makes too much of the idea of equality. The new democracy is not reticent on that question of equality. . . . It will rather proceed to fulfill the nebulous dream . . . , even if the superior people are stript of their superiorities in the process. . . . Even if institutions that betray the people have to go."[9] Reactionary fears lurk beneath Wendell's words when he claims that such rigid interpretations of democracy threaten divine order, the higher ideals of social power. Democracy, he says, has become a "graven image": "we have unwittingly made ourselves idols" (316). Tocqueville, too, warned of the tyrannous majority, and Wendell's defense is not wholly emotional. Social Darwinism hardly encouraged egalitarianism, and American equality always meant, to Wendell, "frank recognition of certain social classes as superior to others. So long as the higher rank was freely accessible to able men of whatever birth and so long as it in no wise empowered those who attained it to transmit their privileges to unworthy descendants" (264). Wendell's democratic ideal means social order and mobility, not social obstruction; and he is fully aware of a democratic problem inherent in the difference between freedom and equality: "However fervently Americans may have believed that all men are created equal, they have never gone so far as to insist that all men must permanently remain so" (267).

The true embodiment of this ideal is Abraham Lincoln; his words about government of, for, and by the people reiterate Wendell's belief that the American ideal means "none unworthily secure" or "undeservedly oppressed" (301) and that Lincoln himself illustrates the American "chiaroscuro appreciation of decent obscurity" (280). While Wendell was unfortunately unable—because of class prejudice or ignorance of actual conditions—to recognize the economic oppression growing in a rapidly industrializing nation, he still defines American government as one "not of authority but of consent"—a government that respects "not the tyranny of any one class over any other, but the consent of all classes—none secured by inflexible privilege—to exist together under a system trusted by all to act as guardian and agent of their common welfare."[10]

The Wendell who despaired about radical contemporary political trends is the late nineteenth-century man of letters caught between the aristocratic, conservative trends of genteel Boston and the expansive, raucous energy of a vigorous nation. Robert Falk says of the genteel critics: "From the social and political desperations of The Gilded Age and Reconstruction decades, American criticism for the most part stood somewhat aloof. It neither espoused a subservience of literature to the business ethics of Jay Gould nor did it strongly champion a collectivist protest against political and economic deviation. Instead it grounded its hopes on a return to an earlier democratic faith that the individual consciousness contained the will and the strength to bring about necessary reforms in society."[11]

This statement characterizes much of Wendell's attitude; for, like many New Englanders, he looked back to an earlier day with nostalgia. But the 1870s and 1880s were the decades of Stedman and Stoddard, and the 1890s according to Wendell in *The Privileged Classes*, faced "the double difficulty that the past is bewildering in its complexity and the future illimitable in its uncertainty" (81). Wendell fully documents the dilemma of writers caught between the fading of the Boston sunset and the still gray dawn of a new day; he clearly realizes the momentousness of his own time as pivotal for the new century: "For on the course which our history takes, more than on anything, must depend the course which must inevitably be taken by the history of the coming world." What that course would be—whether class warfare or the strengthening of imperial democracy—Wendell can never muster the strength to predict; at times he is optimistic, and then again cynical—a mixed state of mind that over and over produces the same metaphor with which he concludes *Liberty, Union, and Democracy:* "When the years to come are past and when those who contemplate the century now beginning can see it in final completeness, the course of the single traditional democracy now existing—of our own America—shall prove most tremendously whether at this moment of crescent democratic force our world is passing into the dusk of a new barbarism or the dawn of a new dispensation" (236–37). Later in his life, Wendell used Joseph Turner's painting *Fighting Téméraire* as an image for his life and the picture of the once gallant old hulk being towed lifeless and useless away beneath a new dawn is once more ambiguous: one does not know whether he sees the ship as the state or as himself, the old man.

V   *The View from Paris*

In *Liberty, Union, and Democracy*, Wendell argues that election is the origin of the American "saving faith in order," and his fear of the mob displaces his early doubts about the benevolent tyranny of the priests. The interrelationship of theological, sociological, political, and historical concerns in *Cotton Mather* typifies Wendell's incessant attention to the national ideals of America; and *The France of Today* (1907) is a book comparable to *Cotton Mather* in the view it provides of Wendell's sociological sensitivity. Less amateurish than *Liberty, Union, and Democracy*, but less valuable in the long run perhaps than *Cotton Mather*, his study of French culture clarifies the popularity Wendell enjoyed in France and demonstrates his continuing appreciation of the motivational force of national idealism.

That the book has importance sociologically is clear not only from its many reprintings from 1907 to 1925 and its Paris publication in 1910, but from the praise of J. J. Jusserand: "I greatly admire the book. . . . He has looked at real France, the France who works, thinks, discovers, teaches, and leads, all told, a rather austere sort of life; he has shown sides of the French character which we never show, which at least our novels never show. His work deserves indeed much praise." No American, he said, "had ever understood the French people as he understood and explained them."[12] The book is also interesting in its appreciation for French life and culture in opposition to the genteel distaste for what Henry James called the French "lightness of soil in the moral region" and the Teutonic, pro-German, racial attitudes of the time. In any case, the French translation of the book, Wendell's honorary degree from France, the lectureship offer from Berlin, and the book's republication in the tense postwar 1920s testify to its value; "coming, as it happened, on the eve of the Great War, the book has an especial significance, and will endure forever, as the best description of the social conditions of France at the outbreak of a momentous struggle."[13] James Hyde in the French version of Mark Howe's biography of Wendell testified to the book's striking importance to the French:

Nul Français ne peut lire ces mots sans un sentiment de fierté, surtout quand il se souvient que ce jugement de Wendell sur la France fut plus que justifié, peu après, par la force et l'endurance extraodinaires avec lesquelles elle résista à la menace de mort que la Guerre Mondiale était pour elle. . . . J'aimerais à croire, et en fait cela m'a été dit par des Français, que c'est à des marques de sympathie et de confiance comme celles de Professeur Wendell donne dans son livre, qu'est du à réveil de l'incomparable esprit de la France qui lui permit dans cette guerre avec l'Allemagne de défendre triomphalment son pays, ses institutions, et sa gloire.[14]

No Frenchman can read these words without a feeling of pride, above all when he remembers that Wendell's judgment of France was more than justified, a little later, by the strength and extraordinary endurance with which she resisted the threat of death posed for her by the World War. . . . I would like to believe, and in fact this has been said to me by Frenchmen, that it is to indications of sympathy and confidence like the ones Professor Wendell gives in his book, which are due the revival of the incomparable spirit of France which allowed her in that war with Germany to triumphantly defend her country, her institutions, and her honor.

William James also praised Wendell's astute "international psychology" and declared it is "not only a good book but a good action."[15]

VI *French Institutions, American Ideals*

Discussing nearly every phase of French society—its education social structure, temperament, family, religion, literature, politics—Wendell's method in *The France of Today*, as in the literary histories, is both analytic and comparative. French education, for instance, is rigorous and serious; its students are less concerned with fact than system and are far better prepared, "in some cases despairingly so," than American students. With regard to the French readiness to "describe themselves as bourgeois" (62), he notes a similar acceptance of the term by the English middle class; and he criticizes the ludicrous American attitude toward equality which creates, in its acceptance of the idea that no man is a superior, "comical" situations, for example, ones wherein "a good Yankee who has made an honest fortune [must share] . . . the aristocratic prejudice of societies which regard the fact that a man is engaged in business as a reason why he should not be invited to dinner" (56).

The Wendell who inveighs against the "insidious" threat to excellence in American democracy praises the strength and vigor of the French middle class. And he does so with the conviction "that the middle class must be the core of any nation, comparatively spared from the over-ripeness of aristocracy, and from the crudity . . . of the masses" (67). With an idealistic feeling for the democratic average man and with a matter-of-fact analytical certainty he regards respectability as "the virtue which . . . has distinguished the middle class of France . . . , the virtue most dear to the middle class of England, as well as to the better sorts of Americans, among whom middle-class manners have grown something like the assurance of aristocratic feeling" (82). During his stay in France, Wendell may have experienced only the bourgeois society of France, but he exhibits a nice awareness of the tensions between aristocratic, artistic, and bourgeois classes (72ff)—while defining his sense of the "better sort"—and a realization that the structure of society in Third Republic France was still rigid (82).

His attention to the French family, highly praised for its incisiveness, makes a distinction between the French and American family habits that is important not only for a comprehension of French life but for an illustration of Wendell's awareness of his own country. The French, he says in a half-hearted nod to Comstockery, "perhaps have strayed further from Eden than we. . . . Among ourselves, no doubt, the ethical ideal is perfection. . . . But, even more surely than we, the French are aware that humanity can never be perfect" (140). Such a statement has many implications: in the first place, the book appeared during the amazing American Age of Innocence, where the ideal of perfectibility seemed increasingly close to reality. But, in broader perspective, the idea Wendell states recalls the American Adam idea—Wendell's belief in what he calls America's "national inexperience," a freedom from, or ignorance of, the harsh backlog of the corrupting institutions of European experience.

Moreover, this statement serves as an important yardstick for measuring some salient differences between French and American life. The French "intellectual candor" which recognizes more willingly the facts of human existence than does the "personal candor" of Americans (150–51) will "plainly set forth a range of human error which the custom and indeed the impulse of [Americans] in similar circumstances would have [been] disposed to ignore or to veil." He states the distinction explicitly: "The French state of mind in this matter has no shade of conscious affrontery; neither has the English or American any conscious tinge of hypocrisy. There is a deep difference, however, between people like ourselves comfortably disposed to believe that things are as they ought to be until the contrary is shown, and people like the French, who frankly recognize that things are as they are" (169). Wendell's distinction is very much like Howells's in his argument that American literature adheres to the clean respectabilities of American life. Wendell's understanding involves aspects of society ranging from divorce to literary expression, augments his pro-French sympathy, and provides testimony against charges of Wendell's narrow scruples and Victorian prudishness.

Wendell may be attempting to argue away any prurience in

French taste when he observes about French literature and its audience that, in the first place, such literature differs from ordinary life and is interesting to the average Frenchman insofar as it represents not the commonplace but the exceptional (236). Such a position, while perhaps true, tends to confirm the suspicion that the only ordinary life in the France of the Third Republic was that of the bourgeois, but it certainly absolves them of the popular nineteenth-century charge of personal licentiousness. On the other hand, Wendell makes a distinction, one rather popular among the "custodians of culture," between the average French and American reader, that what is palatable to one is immoral to the other. "The public to whom French literature is addressed, in short, is always assumed to be mature," and so with the French appreciation of candor: "The difference is that we are disposed to display our reverence for youth by excessive attention to our library shelves and the French display theirs by the more summary process of keeping the library doors shut" (200). He ties these observations into general national tendencies: "Our whole conception of education implies our belief that literature should be addressed to everybody who can and will read it"—especially, of course, the sixteen-year-old schoolgirl. But "their whole conception of education implies their contrary belief that literature should be addressed only to those who have outgrown domestic supervision" (203).

As is characteristic of Wendell's analytical method, he goes beyond any Bostonian prudery to say that the French "think our novels hypocritical, and theirs seem to us corrupt; and both of them are wrong" (220): both views derive from national character and do not necessarily reflect the value of the respective literatures. Indeed, our Boston critic can describe modern French literature as "that great body of literature—in many respects the most admirable of modern times" (197); it reveals a classical awareness of form and care of expression and an effort "not to increase the wealth of society, but to enlarge its intelligence, and above all to intensify its aesthetic pleasure" (229–30). And Wendell can in the days of American neoromantic fiction correctly categorize American literature as "the ephemeral vivacity of popular journalism" (236). This observation is not that of a writer seeking the past, nor even of a man whose critical powers were enervated by the clash of cultures. He condemned contemporary, popular American fiction and praised the very literature that neoromantic critics were claiming American writers had finally gotten out of their blood.

Wendell's discussion, finally, of the French Revolution and the Third Republic once again affords him the opportunity to analyze and compare, to express his convictions about American democracy. The French Revolution, for example, denied the older doctrine of human evil and traditional royal government, whereas the United States maintained the English system of common-law rights, though their revolution nonetheless destroyed much malevolent privilege and repression. Wendell's understanding of the French devotion to philosophical system and intellectual candor explains the continuing governmental crises of the nineteenth century, for both the royal and ecclesiastical tradition of authority and the "philanthropic revolutionary aspirations" still exist in the modern political mind of France. With this conflict in mind, Wendell resorts to the American democratic ideal as a potential resolution of tension in the French Republic: he asserts his own faith in the American belief that "government should derive its just powers from the consent of the governed," by "common consent for the common good" with no class tyranny "high or low, learned or ignorant, few or many" (263).

We can understand French acceptance of Wendell's book since, while he realizes the continuing rigidity of class structure, he maintains that France "has reached a point where . . . reconciliation is no longer inconceivable" (368). He believes that Frenchmen increasingly accept the view "that a truly healthy democracy could never co-exist with a persistent misunderstanding between social classes" (317). The concluding pages present, from a man supposed to have missed the meaning of his country's character, a ringing proclamation of faith in American democracy which "must tolerantly include all manner of men," which must provide the opportunity for a career always to be "open to talent," which must protect against "inherited privilege," and which must allow the pursuit of excellence (374). To Wendell, contemporary France was the collective heritage of the monarchy, the empire, and the republic; of Roland, Saint Louis, Jeanne d'Arc; of the Renaissance and Louis XIV's great century: "all of them together combine to make France great." And he concludes with patriotic optimism: "To the French themselves the Republic still appears not so much national as partisan. I long, with the best of them, for the time when it shall have grown to be no longer partisan, but national; and I believe that time will come" (379).

To conclude our discussion of Wendell's political and social thought with *The France of Today* is to make a bridge between his work as a literary critic and historian, because this work reveals a man less crippled by a conservative fear of the future and by an Adams-like distaste for the present than does the amateurish, captious, often shrill voice of *The Privileged Classes* and *Liberty, Union, and Democracy*. Moreover, it shows a figure less deadened by Tory fears than later critics have remembered. This Wendell is the writer who can render a balanced—if not objective—analysis of contemporary society and who employs a comparative method not to reveal a pro-American or pro-French bias but to illustrate the reasons behind particular national attitudes—traits that, as we shall see, illustrate the structural and historical strength of Wendell's best book, *A Literary History of America*.

In the *France of Today* there is an instructive parallel between the idealistic democrat who finds sterile rigidity in the university, a lack of warmth and communication in social class relationships, a menacing quality in religion, and contradictions in democracy and the man who appeals to national as opposed to sectional, religious, and class prejudices in France: "What matter these dissonances, however, if a tolerable harmony appeared to him to come from the concert of so many diverse voices, and if a rhythm of energy and endurance seemed to animate a France [or America] faithful . . . to its essential virtues?"[16]

We have looked at Wendell's political and social views to clarify our understanding of Wendell's interdisciplinary approach to literary history and criticism. At the same time, however, we have extended the portrait of a varied and complex man. If we have not found the Wendell who, as Horace Traubel claimed, "criticizes the Declaration because it makes too much of the idea of equality,"[17] or who fears that the new democracy "will rather proceed to fulfill the nebulous dream," and thus failed to understand his country, we have found a man of ambivalent faith, one of the "exciting exemplars of conservative political and social thought" in America.[18]

CHAPTER 4

A Literary Historian

THE 1880s witnessed the rise of the modern American university, and Charles W. Eliot's Harvard contributed largely to the emphasis upon the specialized curriculum and upon professional research and scholarship. Barrett Wendell often evinced a hostility to free electives and to the new doctoral degree programs that changed Harvard College into a university. But greater hostility was expressed from outside the universities by critics like Van Wyck Brooks and H. L. Menchen who attacked the isolated, sterile pedantry and irrelevancy of "the professors." The "Band" of genteel writers who have come to represent all that was escapist, romantic, pessimistic, and tender-minded during the last decades of Wendell's career were essentially poets and editors who had more ties to the business world of New York than to the academic world of Cambridge; yet every critic, historian, writer, and professor who failed to denounce the provincial and puritan in American letters or to espouse the cheerful liberation of morals and taste and the freedom of creative intuition and democratic self-expression which the literary radicals of the early twentieth century felt vital for the new era came under the broad attacks aimed at the Genteel Tradition.

Wendell's literary studies certainly seem far removed from the late nineteenth-century literary battles over romanticism, realism, and naturalism. His *Shakspere* (1894) follows the chronology of the playwright's life and the development of his art. *The Temper of the Seventeenth Century in English Literature* (1904), given originally as the Clark Lectures at Trinity College, Cambridge University, pursues the English mind and literature from 1600 to 1700 as they progress from Renaissance "sponteneity," to consciously factual prose, to Puritan "enthusiasm," to Restoration frankness and Dryden's "sanity." *The Traditions of European Literature* (1920) follows century by century the main currents of European writing "from

Homer to Dante." These works, along with his study of American literature which ends essentially in the 1860s, have earned Wendell a modern reputation as an academic representative of the Genteel Tradition. Yet we need to distinguish more carefully than has usually been the case between the magazine tradition of critics like Edmund Clarence Stedman and the academic profession of scholars like Barrett Wendell.

Between William Prescott's *Conquest of Mexico* (1843) and George Lyman Kittredge's *Chaucer and His Poetry* (1915), American scholarship underwent enormous change. Required college curricula in the classical manner became the elective curricula in the modern fashion. By 1900, when Wendell stood at the peak of his career, academic sholarship under the philological and scientific influence of the German universities was becoming more rigorous, more methodological, more objective. Jared Sparks was an impressionistic historian in the romantic school; John Fiske was an evolutionary historian who used the biological theories of Darwin and Spencer; James Russell Lowell was a "humanist"; G. L. Kittredge was a "philologist." For better or worse, the university was beginning to develop a system of specialized, scientific scholarship that to this day is still charged with pedantry and irrelevancy. The academic tradition upholds values of dispassionate, objective investigation and analysis quite different from the impressionistic, aristocratic, escapist values of the Genteel Tradition, though to the disaffected young writers at the beginning of the twentieth century both traditions appeared similar in their debilitating effect upon the would-be artist.

Barrett Wendell also despised the potential sterility of specialized scholarship, though at the same time his studies in composition, Cotton Mather and the early Puritans, and American literature were major contributions to the new university system; for, within that system, he represents the best academic concern for "relevant" scholarship. His composition courses were a mecca for the embryonic artist; he constantly admonished young writers to draw their material from the reality of life around them; and he therefore stands between the charges on one side of academic isolationism and on the other side of genteel escapism. His repeated goal was for students to "think things together," and the extent of his success is our concern in chapter 7. We have already surveyed Wendell's attention to the political and social values of his day, even though temperamentally he found the modern world distasteful; we shall see too his serious efforts to write a cultural essay on the American temper and its art. But Wendell himself summarized the thrust of his career:

Nobody knows better than I that I am no scholar—and therefore of no consequence to learning. Yet one thing I did in my teaching seems to me right. I tried to make pupils read things, and not weight their unsteady heads with things that had been written about things—historic, linguistic, whatever else. My task as a Harvard teacher was to give glimpses of literature to men who could generally not be concerned with it in practical life. That I never forgot. Any scholar can help make scholars; but lots fail in the process to humanize. My real duty, as I saw it, was not scholarly but humane.[1]

Wendell admired the classical orientation of Lowell, but he recognized in it a superficiality. He feared the narrow pedantry of the new philology, but he respected its depth of insight. Torn in conflicting directions, Wendell self-consciously opted for the past, and called himself a dilletantish man of letters rather than a scholarly man of learning. But, at the same time, his writing, albeit marred by his temperamental biases, reveals an indebtedness to the scholarship of his day. Like his former professor Charles Eliot Norton, Wendell's concern is often less with the art itself than with art as an expression of the age. He is realistic and objective; he is an aesthetician and a humanist; he is idealistic and impressionistic; his scholarship is romantic and scientific. Between the extreme impressionism and pedantic scholarship of his day, we may find Wendell's work an empty compromise; it may illustrate the infamous genteel confusion of values; but, more accurately, it should be viewed as Wendell's honest efforts to synthesize the positive features of humanistic and academic traditions.

Wendell's "method" in two ways employs a form of scientific criticism. In the first place, he is a literary historian who is concerned with sources and traditions, with the political events and social milieu which rest behind the artist and his work. If his sociological sensitivity is weak, he nonetheless seeks actively to understand the productive forces, the standards, and criteria of the past. At the same time, he structures the movement of literature according to a form of literary social Darwinism; as a former student recalled, he held "fast to the principles of evolution as opposed to

revolution."[2] But, as we shall see, Wendell is not a scientific historian; his sense of values, his aesthetic sense, and his personal fears
intrude throughout his historical studies; and, as a result, his criticism is also "a kind of personal imaginative association that is not
closely allied to law-giving criticism."[3]

The New Humanists could find much to admire in Wendell's use
of history—if not because of any sense of "inner check," at least
through his sympathy and selection among the touchstones of the
Greek and Christian past. Irving Babbitt's appreciation of a knowledge of the classics as well as an understanding of the relevance of
the present might well describe, for instance, Wendell's purpose in
The Traditions of European Literature, in which his objective "was
at once to revive knowledge which was sinking beneath the level of
[modern] consciousness" and to do so because "the classics, ancient
and modern, have slowly revealed themselves as standards of perception; whoever comes to know them has a measure by which he
can test or correct his impulsive judgment concerning new works of
literature."[4]

Wendell's concern involves the humanistic effort to discern with
reason and imagination between historical fact and human values,
and he indicates something of this stance in his review of Edward
Eggleston's *The Transit of Civilization:* "The historian of a past
civilization must somehow bring himself into imaginative sympathy
with the human spirit of the times with which he deals, until he
understands not only bare facts but also how those facts made the
living men feel who knew them in the flesh."[5] Repeatedly, in letters, lectures, and books, Wendell argues for the method that led to
Harvard's honors degree in history and literature. This method attempted to get students to "think facts together," the task "not of
accumulation but of synthesis . . . , based on facts but facts thought
together," the data of literature and history "perceived in their
mutual relations."

I *Race, Place, Moment*

Hippolyte Taine's influence on American literary studies in the
late nineteenth century has often been noted, and Harry Hayden
Clark has observed that Wendell's "very influential *Literary History
of America* (1900) was partly influenced by Taine."[6] Wendell in
France of Today admitted to finding Taine "admirable," "always
precise, always intelligent, and above all incessantly suggestive"

(293). The organization by century Wendell gives his material in the *Literary History*, in the study of seventeenth-century literature, and in *The Traditions of European Literature* represents what René Wellek calls a "time section defined by a system of norms embedded in the historical process and irremovable from it."[7] The "temper," then, of seventeenth-century English literature has importance not only because of the literature per se, not merely because of the historical and religious struggles of the century, but because it reflects through the works of Shakespeare, Milton, and Dryden the shifting values of Elizabethan, Puritan, and Restoration England (England past and England future), and at the same time reveals the values and characteristics of those pioneer forefathers of America. Wendell repeatedly employs Taine's concept of "moment," of the spirit of an age, to structure his historical concerns; thus he is able to compare and contrast precursors and successors within a national, religious, or imaginative progression. Wendell conceived of literature as a "temperamental fact," valuable historically and psychologically for its "human rhythm," and its reflection of the national "moment" which produced it. Literature to Wendell, as for Taine, was a "part of the general historical process conceived as an organized unity."[8]

We may study this method in greater detail by looking at his historical studies. His *Shakspere*, for example, aims at a coherent view of the poet's life and works, an attempt like his study of Cotton Mather to see Shakespeare "as he saw himself," which means analyzing the "commonplaces of human experience," the Elizabethan drama, its audience, and its stage.[9] As Wendell remarked in his Renaissance course, "the drama, like Shakspere himself, was no isolated phenomenon. . . . Our problem is to discover what life was like to those old Englishmen of three centuries ago. Like all literature and all art, what records they have left us are valuable . . . chiefly as comments on life as significant as to the facts behind them."[10] We learn variously then of the vice-ridden low-life of dramatists, of Shakespeare's emergence from that life to success, and of his death finally as a "gentleman."

Henry IV serves as a reflector both of the low-life taverns Shakespeare knew and of the better life achieved by success (172). Wendell illustrates the Elizabethan "taste for verbal novelty" with John Lyly's *Euphues* (29) and the delight in experimentation with Edmund Spencer's *The Shepherd's Calendar* (30); and in *King Lear* he finds

74 BARRETT WENDELL

Shakespeare catering to a public taste for rant without sacrificing propriety. Shakespeare's *Troilus and Cressida* also contains the "sonorous rant and prolonged soliloquy" more appreciated by sixteenth-century than by nineteenth-century audiences. The ghosts, spirits, and witches which increasingly fill Shakespeare's plays around 1600 reflect Shakespeare's growing interest in the occult. And Wendell prefaces each discussion of a play with source information and comment on the degree to which Shakespeare was imitative.

Wendell at last observes that the imaginative facts of Shakespeare's career augment the few records we have of his life, and Wendell's purpose is to keep in mind that, "in admiration for the aspects in which, from time to time, that genius defines itself, people may fatally forget the truth that Shakspere's work really emanated from a living man" (397). In some cases, it is difficult to accept what Wendell believes deductively to have been acceptable to Elizabethans (such as his belief that Lear was meant to be comic, not tragic [292]). His remarks on Shakespeare's creative improvement of his sources proves more informative; but, as we shall see, he appears most effective about the evolution of Shakespeare's genius.

Wendell's concerns in *Traditions of European Literature* are clearly broader than in his book on Shakespeare, but the sweep of literature from the perspective of the whole of Western civilization mirrors the same evolutionary law of Shakespeare's career. In this work, he makes a more concrete use of the historical method—each section begins with a chapter on "Historical Traditions"—and he continually relates the events of history to the literature. The mood of Rome and Ovid's personal situation relate, for instance, to his *Metamorphoses;* the reign of Frankish kings and the battle of Ronceveaux are used in the *Song of Roland;* the medieval church, Saint Thomas, and the troubadours are all essential to Dante's *Divine Comedy*. Overall, however, his historical concerns with European traditions as something directly antecedent to the present are clearly central; like Ferdinand Brunetière, he seems to feel that the greatest influence on any book may be another book: the eleventh book of the *Odyssey* with Odysseus's trip to the underworld inevitably precedes the same journey of Aeneid in the *Divine Comedy*. The Pindaric ode strongly influences Abraham Cowley, William Wordsworth, Samuel Coleridge, James R. Lowell; and the Horatian ode provides the "grand precedent" for English neoclassical poetry

(246). "That Herrick could not have existed without Jonson is evident; no more could Jonson have existed without Martial" (310). And discussing the Roman traditions, the classical ideas of the Roman Empire, he discovers expression of a basically human desire for "peace by . . . righteous power." He is not the genteel critic who admires the Teutonic as opposed to Latin culture when he reveals the humanist concern to talk of both Roman history and its relevance: "we of the twentieth century need only watch how men are trying to establish a League of Nations to be sure that . . . this ideal is living still" (346).

With the exception of Wendell's *Literary History*, his *Temper of the Seventeenth Century in English Literature* remains his most fascinating and certainly his most eccentric volume. His interest in the "national temper" of seventeenth-century literature develops around the same thesis employed in the *Literary History*. The Elizabethan traits of "spontaneity, enthusiasm, and versatility," coupled with Puritan theology, produced the trauma of civil war as well as the greatness of Milton and the reaction of Restoration in England. Renaissance vitality and integrity disintegrated in the face of political, religious, and scientific controversy into an increasing self-consciousness and the deliberate expression of men "who sought, or who were driven into, personal isolation."[11]

The violence of national discord and the sense of personal solitude appeared partially as a function of rising Puritanism and served as a historical metaphor for Calvinist doctrine: "The solitude of Milton is rather the inevitable solitude of his disintegrating time," as well as his Puritan "seriousness and austerity" (295, 301). In both "Lycidas" and *Paradise Lost,* Wendell finds the creative genius of the "one true poet of the national disintegration of England"—"grave, lofty, austere, deliberate, noble, and blind" (316, 326). With the Restoration, then, came a resurgence, a reintegration of national and literary feeling, a temper formed by release from abstract principle as the basis for political and social order. The spontaneous Englishman of 1600 had become by 1700 the Whig—tenacious, "rigidly polite and cool," and addicted to the couplet (334, 351). The dashing quality of a Sir Philip Sidney or Sir Walter Raleigh gave way to Roger de Coverley and the John Bull character, a temper Wendell could still see as a British characteristic in 1902.

Wendell's method is explicitly historical, even though he inveighs against that method in the opening pages: "In this scientific age, the orthodox way is doubtless to deal with [men and books] as facts, inquiring what influences and what surroundings produced this book or that" (3). He intends, however, to avoid that "admirable orthodoxy," to approach literature neither as historical fact nor as aesthetic, but as temperamental fact. But he cannot speak of national temper without reference to historical fact; and the central data—just as it is in his *Liberty, Union, and Democracy* and in his *Literary History*—is Puritanism.

His analysis of this religious force is comprehensive, intelligible, sympathetic, and suggestive. Not only does he celebrate the imaginative strength of the Puritans, but he also reveals his eclectic manner of appropriating salient aspects from contemporary intellectual currents of thought when he finds a significant parallel between the ideas of Puritan doctrine and the beliefs of Spencerian and Darwinian science: the survival of the fittest represents the scientific view of the election of God's chosen; and Puritan strength resides, then, for Wendell in the "theological correlation of biological fact" (220, 227–28), despite the fact that theological election is eternal and biological survival of the individual momentary. Still while his specific analysis of the Puritan faith correctly locates its rise as one of the central historical, political, and literary facts of the seventeenth century, his application of general evolutionary principles in the development of his history attracts attention to the book.

II *Evolutionary Criticism*

Certainly the work of evolutionists like Brunetière, Darwin, Spencer, and Fiske figured prominently in the intellectual life of the late nineteenth century. Donald Pizer explicitly analyzes the merging of Taine's sense of milieu with the evolutionary science of Darwin and Spencer to forge the scientific concerns of Howells, T. S. Perry, Hamlin Garland, and many other critics of the 1880s. Pizer points out that "academic critics . . . did not go to the extreme of building evolutionary critical systems,"[12] but certain tenets were generally and clearly accepted by both magazine and academic critics: literature, conceived as a product of society, was, like society, continually in flux; and it evolved in two ways—progressively (and for some Darwinian critics, competitively) through its socially determined origins, and cyclically (in the older terms of Johann Herder and Friedrich Schlegel, growth, proliferation, maturity, decay) through its particular genre.

While individual literary genres moved inevitably through the birth-death pattern giving way subsequently to another genre or a new variant of the same kind, social progress continued from the communal to the individual, the homogeneous to heterogeneous, the simple to the complex, the undifferentiated to the differentiated; and both aspects of evolution show progression from general and abstract through particular and concrete to limitation and artifice. Therefore, in *The Temper of the Seventeenth Century* Wendell talks of "how imagination breaks the limits of old conventions, and of how, after the brief period when imagination and sense of fact have been immortally fused, a crushing sense of fact slowly and inexorably checks the further aspirations of imagination, imposing new conventions on an art which is no longer free" (50).

His *Traditions of European Literature* reveals probably less indebtedness to evolutionary criticism than his Shakespeare and seventeenth-century studies, but he does make use of a primary tool in scientific criticism—the comparative method, finding analogous patterns of development in various national artistic traditions.[13] The increased human sympathy, for instance, in Sophocles' treatment of subject as opposed to Aeschylus's attitudes is paralleled by earlier and Periclean Greek sculpture, and by English drama under Elizabeth and that under James I. Furthermore, the difference between Aeschylus, Sophocles, and Euripides is an evolutionary one: Aeschylus neglects the human element in tragedy, Sophocles balances the human with the fateful, and Euripides more expressly deals with human qualities (91). Wendell characteristically, however, leaves ambiguous which of these three is the greatest, thereby disregarding the more assertive evaluation made by Thomas Perry (for example) when he designates Sophocles best by virtue of his intermediate position. Nevertheless, the efforts of Rome to emulate Greece, of Renaissance England to emulate Rome and Athens, of postrevolutionary America to emulate Britain mark evolutionary parallels in the history of European literature (224). Early experimental successes lead to the production of later masterpieces which in turn, as models for imitation, became "tyrants that die hard" (119).

If the evolutionary principles play a secondary role in Wendell's more straightforward chronology in *The Traditions of European Literature*, the whole development of *Shakspere* and *Temper of the Seventeenth Century* is governed by a scientific system. Following

the lead of John Addington Symonds's rigorous description of the
biological development of Elizabethan drama. Wendell in *Shakspere* calls Elizabethan drama "one of the most completely typical
phenomena in the whole history of the fine arts. It took little
more than half a century to emerge from an archaic tradition, to
develop into great imaginative vitality, and to decline into a formal
tradition" (2)—"a remarkably typical example of artistic evolution"
(401). And this development occurred at a time when England as a
nation was emerging from the simple medieval into the complex
modern world, from a homogeneously provincial to a heteroge-
neously imperial power. He finds then conditions satisfying both
aspects of evolution, social and generic. Shakespeare's career, too,
Wendell finds to correspond exactly, in its rise and fall, to the
national drama; he "worked with instinctive fidelity to the greater
laws which govern actual life" (397).

To illustrate the fact of Shakespeare's development, Wendell
stresses four periods in the poet's career: a period of early experimentation; one of increasing imaginative force; a high period of
fused imaginative, spiritual, and psychological force; and a period of
decline. In such a study, the chronology of Shakespeare's plays
becomes of obvious importance; and the words "growth," "maturity," "decline" figure prominently in Wendell's analysis of separate
plays within that chronology. For example, *Two Gentlemen of Ve-
rona* reveals originality and versatility of character in Shakespeare's
"apprenticeship" (101); *Midsummer Night's Dream* demonstrates
an increasing concentration of his power with concrete words (215);
Hamlet, Lear, Othello illustrate "tremendous power both of will and
artistic expression" (339); and in the *Tempest* and *Winter's Tale* the
"old spontaneous power was fatally gone" (387). The major weakness
in Wendell's criticism of Shakespeare arises as a function of this
pattern of cyclical evolution; for, while there is little with which to
quarrel in his understanding of the early and mature plays, Wendell
in illustrating the poet's declining powers does damage to the
strength of the last plays. But the organic theory most attracts our
attention to the book; for, as an early *Dial* reviewer remarked, the
book, while "neither an exposition of the Shakespearian theory of
the conduct of life, nor a statement of the Shakespearian practice [in
dramatic technique], does give us a conception . . . of the growth of
the poet's genius."[14]

Wendell also enunciates a theory of evolutionary thought in *Traditions of European Literature:* artistic growth is characterized by rough experimental forms which break the bounds of an outworn tradition; these then give way to a consummate artistic expression, which give way in turn to forms that are artificial and sterilely imitative of a new convention created by the earlier successful expression. His theoretic observations cohere very closely to the metaphorical if not scientific use of evolutionary thought by writers like Brunetière. Moreover, they figure prominently in both the overall organization and sectional development of *The Temper of the Seventeenth Century in English Literature*, though here as with the *Shakspere*, where his central concern was with the man, Wendell's primary interest, despite his historical and evolutionary organization, is a definition of the temper of seventeenth-century literature.

Wendell rather closely parallels the scientific criticism of Brunetière, who is like Taine in his emphasis on "moment," like Hegel in his view of evolution as action and reaction, and like Darwin in his conception of genres as biologically active. Wendell argues that the simplicity of the laboratory with its ordered laws may not have the same significance as actual reality, but he echoes Brunetière when he says that the "accidents of chronology rarely combine with accidents of expression to define such generalities" (49). Wendell's own work then becomes a creative act, a kind of supreme fiction when he posits English drama of the late sixteenth and early seventeenth century as a case history wherein "we may perceive how any school of art—Greek sculpture . . . , Gothic architecture, Florentine or Venetian painting—rises, flourishes, and decays" (47).

Elizabethan drama broke the bonds of older convention with Christopher Marlowe's mighty line and was enfranchised by the enthusiasm, spontaneity, and versatility of Shakespeare, a man of his time whose work displayed the national temper of his era. But later, "when self-consciousness begins to be inhibitory, when every effort seems to be a conscious one to struggle against the tightening force of new bonds" (85), disintegration began. The earlier feeling of imaginative and spiritual freedom began to encounter limits; for, while a greater rigidity of subject, form, and style crept into the scene with Ben Jonson, his visual imagination shows him "at heart a painter" (67). But, by the closing of the theaters in 1642, the decline

marked by John Webster, John Marston, John Ford, and Thomas
Middleton was complete. The "monstrosity" of their tragic innovations, the "conscious obscenity" of the comedy, the exhaustion of
excessiveness, the exaggeration at the expense of truth in characterization, and the "sinking" of blank verse to the level of rhetoric
pronounced drama dead though not extinct before politics closed its
stage (98).

In seventeenth-century poetry, Wendell follows the same method to somewhat different conclusions. He is of course using generic
criticism in the sense that, as one literary form declined, others
arose to take its place. His use of historical background as well as the
concept of competitive evolution heightens the drama of the fading
stage, the rising poetry, the juvenescent prose; and he uses more
generally evolutionary standards, the older organological method,
when he traces the history of the lyric through its rise in Thomas
Wyatt, the Earl of Surrey, and Michael Drayton; its climax in Jonson, Spenser, and John Donne; and its decline in William Browne,
Phineas Fletcher, and George Wither. In the "Italianate grace" of
Spenser, in the "civility of Jonson's classical poise," and in the
"affectations of a mannerism" in Donne lay the seeds of decline
which appear in the lifeless imitation of the Spenserians, the Sons of
Ben, and the Metaphysicals.

Wendell's analysis of particular poets in these various schools
always leaves much to be desired by way of supportive specificity,
but his concern with each poet, he says, is rather "to perceive his
relation, on the whole, to his fellows" (102). He is content briefly to
point out imitation and not individuality as salient in poets like
Browne, John Suckling, George Herbert. By the time he gets to
William Davenant and Abraham Cowley, he finds only "sham" and
"ingenious excesses" (146).

Unlike the drama, however, which had effectively faded by the
appearance of James Shirley's work into decadence, the
seventeenth-century lyric "never sunk into a state of repellent decay" (152). The work of Robert Herrick and Henry Vaughan still
showed strength despite the demise of the old robust manner, the
national integrity of Elizabeth's reign. The poetry genre faded but
soon found new vigor, a new elevation in the Puritan genius of
Milton. The midcentury temper of the seventeenth century, which
could not be expressed in drama, could find a new voice in the
increasing sense of personal isolation born of political and theologi-

cal conflict. However, Wendell feels that seventeenth-century prose demonstrates the rising genre most characteristic of the changing national temper.

Elizabethan prose displayed little more than experimental, unmemorable efforts; but between 1600 and 1650, as drama and poetry began to decline, English prose "developed a new power" (162). Wendell sees in the dissolution of poetry and drama the fading traits of the Elizabethan era; and the nascent English temper of the seventeenth century, which culminated in eighteenth-century neoclassicism, is reflected by prose—the genre best fitted to the needs of the changing temper. The works of Thomas Overbury, John Earle, and Thomas Fuller never achieved eminence, but they "remain historically important" because they mark the course which English literature took "on its way from the unreal conventions of Elizabethan satire to the crescent vitality of Addison" (168).

But that "minor prose" leaves Wendell with Walter Raleigh, the King James Bible, Francis Bacon, Robert Burton, and Thomas Browne to account for. And the way he analyzes their work in terms of his theory of genre development is ingenious but strained. The spirit of the time was conducive to masterful translations like the Bible, to works like Bacon's "masterpieces of proverbial wisdom," and to Raleigh's world history of "half-repressed imaginative fervor" (190–92). But, while this prose thus developed in range, power, and variety, it "had not reached the momentary stability of so fixed a manner as should inevitably impose itself on the writings to come" (191). That is, English prose of the first half-century proved great, but not because it reflected the changing English temper; it introduced a marvelous vehicle of carefully specified meaning. But, in terms of genre development, it failed because the creative mood was still largely imaginative and not yet balanced sufficiently by the factual. Implicit here, of course, is the growing scientific revolution of the seventeenth century which at first caused debilitating conflicts for the early prose writers but which finally emerged preeminent as the ultimate vehicle of its expression struggled through its embryonic phase.

Within this organic and generic evolutionary frame, Wendell describes the temper underlying the literature: Burton appears less significant an artist, but he is more specifically in tune with the growing mood "toward no too buoyant a view of life" (193)—one clearly reflected in Burton's melancholy humor. When Bacon and

Raleigh tried to weave the learning of their day into prose, they "only revealed its poverty." The lingering Elizabethan imaginative enthusiasm, Burton's "hodge-podge" and his "garrulous pedantry," also reflect "the normal mood of learning" in his time (197). In Browne, Wendell sees even additional reflections of the national temper, if nonetheless by a reaction against it; what distinguishes Browne in the face of the immense contemporary conflicts, at a time when "'tis all in pieces, all coherence gone," is his "constantly deliberate care for every syllable" (201). In a world in which "fierce abandonment of deliberation" reigned, narrowness of scope and precise rhetoric became almost personal necessities. While the prose of 1600 "seems national," that of Browne's and Burton's "seems deliberately individual" (209).

René Wellek notes in his discussion of Brunetière's theories of literary evolution that they display both a metaphoric sense of evolutionary rise and decay and a Darwinian sense of increasingly differentiated development.[15] Both senses characterize Wendell's use as we have so far seen it here. Moreover, we must remember that the critical approach operates for Wendell in the service of a larger, more imaginative purpose. Evolutionary structure for him is merely a handy but arbitrary tool; the patterned development which it uncovers in Shakespeare and in the literature of the seventeenth century is not the trait which has made the literature survive, as he makes clear in *Shakspere:* "Just now the study of literary evolution happens to be in question, or at least appeal to the temper of the day. The temper in question is now and probably transient" (419).

His attention is always more immediately concerned with national and individual temper and ideals. His demonstration of declining poetic and dramatic expression in the 1600s and of emerging prose serves to illustrate primarily the change from the integration of national feeling in Elizabethan England to the increasing mood of individual isolation in Milton. The inevitable clash of a Catholic temper with the Puritan personal temper was both historical and literary. It created the Civil War, the Protectorate, and Milton whose mood combined masterfully the cosmic and lyric power of the Renaissance with the personal, spiritual intensity of the Reformation. Yet prose, not poetry, was the emergent literary form because a new national temper was forged in the fires of political rebellion, scientific innovation, and royal restoration; for, while Milton supremely expressed individuality and isolation, his period in the century marked one of spiritual disintegration which gave way to a new national integrity in the age of Dryden, an age which demanded and welcomed the exercise not of repressive religious attraction but shrewd common sense. What Wendell describes finally as characteristic at the end of the seventeenth century is an "impulse, more mature than that of elder times, to recognize and respect plain fact, and to hold that ideals are things essentially apart, not to be ignored or neglected, but not to be confused with the inevitable circumstance of material existence" (345). Wendell feels that in science the new age (of Robert Boyle, Isaac Newton, and John Locke) was far more remarkable than in literature; and so the commonsense England of John Bull diverged increasingly from the still idealistic, sheltered colonies in the New World.

III *The Individual Talent*

Wendell is concerned, therefore, with more than evolution—the rise and fall of genres or the competition among them—in his histories. In *Shakspere*, he notes the "strange, mysterious strength" of Shakespeare's creative imagination which existed before and shall exist after the fad of evolution; "for what makes him perennial is that . . . he is a man of genius" (419). A major position of evolutionary criticism diminished the role of the author's creative genius; and Howells called the romantic cult of genius "mischievous superstition." Indeed, the scientific determinism of the evolutionary stance brought the newer critic into major conflict with the romantic theory of the creative artist. As a result of this view of the author, Thomas Perry could admit that Sophocles, Shakespeare, and Dante no doubt displayed genius but that their achievement appeared not so much a personal one as the necessary result of their relative position "in the development of their genres."

Here we see the double-sided Wendell again: he employs the scientific method but tempers it with an older, more subjective appreciation, or perhaps a newer one—since critical impressionism and attention to genius (in the sense of craft, not personality) helped lay to rest the evolutionary school of literary history in the 1920s. In Wendell's *Shakspere*, the stage, the dramatic forces of early Elizabethan England, the sources at Shakespeare's disposal, the Renaissance temper are all important for Wendell; but they never explain that other force, Shakespeare's genius. While a large part of Edward Dowden's *Mind and Art* (1875) dealt with Shakespeare's

mind, Wendell is more concerned with his art. Despite the typical
artistic evolution found in Elizabethan drama and in the "normality"
of Shakespeare's artistic growth, the fact remains to Wendell that
Shakespeare is an "artist of first-rate genius" whose work tends to
make us "forget that it was made for any other conditions than those
amid which, generation after generation, we find it" (2–3). Shakespeare transcends "trivial history"; and Wendell, rather than being
the scientific devotee of Taine or Brunetière (though the latter's
Hegelian sense clearly allowed for genius), tends toward the
humanistic and aesthetic in his definition of Shakespeare's talent;
indeed, he finds Coleridge's estimates of Shakespeare, though at
times "queerly erratic," to be "interesting" and "lasting" (396–97).

Critics in the Genteel Tradition, like E. C. Stedman, promoted
the idea shared by Wendell that the final test of any art lies in its
execution; but their concept of the natural aptitude of the artist and
his ability to see a divine unity beyond ordinary reality was more
transcendental than Wendell's attitude. He is enough of an aesthetician, as a teacher of composition, to assert the importance of artistic craft-consciousness; but his romantic predilections led him to believe that a great deal of Shakespeare's genius resided in his innate
ability to cross the metaphoric gap between the world and man's
linguistic symbols for that world. At the same time, his chronological study of Shakespeare attempts to show the poet's growing mastery over his medium. Both impressionistic and formalistic, then,
Wendell talks of Shakespeare's genius as strange and mysterious, as
creative of more than it knew, and as productive of characters
beyond the poet's conscious control (150). There is something
clearly Wordsworthian in the half-perceived, half-created nature of
Wendell's observation about the sonnets as illustrative of Shakespeare's "double personality" which "must first experience his emotion, must then abstract himself from it" (228).

Part of that duality has neurotic aspects for Wendell. He evokes
an ancient attitude toward the artist when he speaks of the "divine
madness," the mental activity verging on madness, so clearly at
work in Shakespeare's great tragedies; but "the trait which balanced
his abnormal activity of intellectual perception was an equally active
and pervasive power of reflection" (258). This view in Wendell's
criticism is hardly restricted to Shakespeare, since, for instance, he
saw Jonathan Swift's work as a product of mania and will. In Shakespeare, he describes the substance of this mysterious combination in

personal terms: it consists of a sympathy for the "depths of human suffering"; a sense—especially in *Othello* and *Macbeth*—of the constant irony and "constant trouble which surrounds the fact of woman"; and in the great tragedies *Lear* and *Hamlet* a "deep sympathy with . . . abnormal, overwrought states of mind" (338–39).

IV *Impressionism, Expressionism*

Wendell's critical approach moves between romantic impressionism—or as he said "dilettantish" criticism—and scientific criticism, what he called "pedantic scholarship." At times, his concern is clearly impressionistic: he would rather discuss what literature "seems" to each reader; for, as he told his students, "If your impression and mine agree, each can feel the surer; if they differ, each is safer from the infatuating temptation of self-sufficiency. Meanwhile, if we have discussed only our impressions we have violated no privacy, cross-questioned no tender reserve."[16] As a result, we read of the "perennial delights" of Shakespeare; we are told to "try only to feel as [Dante] felt, in the sunset of the middle age"; and we learn that Shakespeare's style in *Lucrece* is "a euphuistic antithesis between the hardness of marble and the softness of wax." Many times, when discussing the effect of some work which arises "we know not how," Wendell cannot even find words adequate to the impression.

Yet by no means can we regard Wendell as merely impressionistic, for "the final test of fine art is to be found in its own inherent beauty," its unified expression of lasting meaning. Wendell's values are not the aesthetics, bordering on "art for art's sake," of the Genteel Tradition, but they are more nearly those of the New Humanists, since the best art, to Wendell, is a well-executed articulation of life's meaning, worth, and tragedy. What he meant by "beauty" involved his reaction against sterile pedantry in scholarship: "the method of Wendell's critical thoughts [was] that all his teaching of literature is based on examination of the extent of the whole. There is no captious picking at detail, no isolation of a part, to which the 'academic mind' is unhappily prone; a book, a poem, is a rounded whole—or nothing."[17]

From his approach to the artist's work as a whole, Wendell posits an essentially aesthetic theory. He would tell a class "that in a work which is excellent as a whole [particular] passages do not stand out. In such work each part fits its place so perfectly that at first it seems wholly to belong there."[18] One student recalled Wendell's byword in composition: "The best style is that which most completely expresses the thought," for Wendell "had no use for verbal decoration that was not structural."[19] In his *English Composition*, this interdependency of form and content with Wendell's "style and thought" is clear; and, where Henry James uses the word "execution," Wendell writes "adaptation": "the more exquisitely style is adapted to the thought it symbolizes, the better we can make our words and compositions denote and connote in other human minds the meaning they denote and connote in ours."[20]

Though Wendell seldom had space to fully develop his concept of this interrelationship of parts, he is concerned, repeatedly in the Shakespeare study, with the manner in which Shakespeare's "absurd" complications of plot are balanced with the reality of his characters: how, for instance, these elements in *As You Like It* are balanced by an atmosphere "consistent with both" (203); how a conventional "tragedy of blood" like *Hamlet* achieves its effect because of the strength and individuality of character, the dramatic and realistic motivation of action (252–53); how contrived devices of identity in *Love's Labour's Lost* and *Comedy of Errors* hurt the play through implausible and inconsistent characterization (96); and how in *Midsummer Night's Dream* scene, plot, character coalesce to produce an "artistic unity" (106).

Part of the difficulty Wendell has with Donne, William Blake, Robert Browning, and Whitman is aesthetic; their "eccentric writing . . . obviously interposes itself between our wits and the meaning which we are trying to comprehend." While Wendell expresses admiration for their content, he asserts that it lacks that vital and necessary "fusion" with form.[21] For Wendell, while enjoyment is the "first and last condition of understanding," the plausibility of plot, consistency of characterization, and appropriateness of style are as prominent aspects of his "poetics" as real life was the touchstone of inspiration for the would-be novelists.

For Wendell, in any case, the omission of attention to the whole in favor of minute detail is the cardinal critical sin. When he evaluates a given work, the facts-imagination dichotomy assumes new dimensions: Wendell apparently disagrees with the evolutionary critics in his belief that the declining, and not the rising, stage of organic progression demonstrates increasing complexity and particularity. But what he means when he says that the late Elizabethans produced a literature in decline, as the results of a "crushing sense of fact," is not that the literature had attained an inevitable stage of specificity but rather that as a literature declines the delicate fusion of imagination and fact and of style and thought dissolves as imaginative power weakens. As writers follow slavishly the fact of older form, experience "begins to check the wilder impulses of creative innovation"; and, as the world becomes too much with us, "nothing is finally fused" (411), and art lapses into convention (402). Whereas Shakespeare's special genius lies in his close mental association of facts, concepts, and words, his late plays suffer from the "inhibitory sense" of fact as he struggles with experimental and fanciful forms; the sense of fact, the oppressive omnipresence of a new, changing world, appear in the technical deliberateness of these plays as Shakespeare's imagination could no longer fuse, for instance, the imaginative world of the *Tempest* (376).

Wendell writes in *The Temper of the Seventeenth Century*, "We should ourselves be anachronisms" in a scientific era of "receding chaos" if we were content only to enjoy "the splendidly confused creations of the art we love" and if we did not "eagerly strive to perceive and to define the relations in which they really stand to one another" (49). An awareness of "inexorable order" is the product of the historian's effort to think things together; and those things are the historical facts of moment—the Pax Romana, the Elizabethan stage, civil war, Puritanism, slave economy—and the order these facts assume generally for Wendell is evolutionary. Pressures both from social movement and individual genius come to bear on the evolutionary cycles, however; and Wendell reflects not only Taine and Brunetière in his systematic history but Sainte-Beuve in his attention to biography and the personality—the psychology of the individual artist—a sometimes confused stance combining elements of the "poeta nascitus" and the poet environmentally determined.

One aspect of the larger cultural patterns revealed by the individual writer is national temper; and the "inextricably intermingled" facts of national temper, individual artist, social milieu, and literary tradition in Wendell's theory is summarized by René Wellek: "The sciences of culture . . . are interested in the concrete and individual. Individuals, however, can be discovered and comprehended only in reference to some scheme of values, which is merely another name for culture."[22] The shifting emphasis in Wendell's "system" may derive from the circuitous nature of such cultural interdependency, or perhaps from Wendell's distrust of single-minded criticism as opposed to a critical eclecticism and an intellectual openness.

V *American Critical Tradition*

While Wendell never explicitly enunciated his theoretical position, our inductive analysis of his method demonstrates his eclectic participation in many aspects of the critical scene in his day. The movement in American literary criticism from Lowell and Whitman to T. S. Eliot is far more complex than the familiar battle for realism, the genteel adulation of beauty, the liberal reaction against Victorian prudery, or aesthetic humanism in the 1920s—though certainly these facets mark the general outline of seventy years of criticism. From the historical, aesthetic criticism of Lowell, the critical path runs through the optimism of Spencerian evolution where men like James, Howells, and Sidney Lanier sought a romantic vision of reality; through the highwater mark of realism in the 1880s which championed the democratic average in American life; through the collectivist and utopian concerns of Howells, Garland, and Frank Norris to the neoromantic revival and poetry revolution before World War I. The basic critical thrust in these decades came between Stedman's genteel devotees of beauty, culture, and business; Howell's school of realism, democracy, and progress; Babbitt's ethical and classical humanism; Brooks's cultural revivalism; and Henry James's high craftsmanship.

George Santayana's initial use of the phrase "the Genteel Tradition" in attacking the New Humanism is more accurate for locating Wendell than is the confused use of that phrase by later critics: the Genteel Tradition as it has come to designate writers like Stedman, Stoddard, Gilder, Boker, Aldrich, and Taylor spoke for conventionality and correctness; it promoted a romantic, idealistic status quo that led to early attacks on the Puritan tradition and later on the thesis of realism and naturalism. From the pages of the big magazines the genteel writers erected a defense of manners, property, and middle-class taste against the chaos and change of the last half of the nineteenth century. They looked to the English romantics for inspiration, and, as magazine editors, they enforced the now infamous "feminine" and didactic moral standards.

Wendell's snobbish class-consciousness was more Boston Brahmin than New York stockbroker; for a gentleman revealed himself far less by form than by inner substance. He criticized the unrestrained free thought of transcendentalism, especially as it threatened the sense of order inherited from New England Puritanism. While he believed that literature must be taught as it relates to "wholesome" life, he depised the "fastidious overrefinement," the euphemism of contemporary literature, and urged his students to see life steadily and whole. He looked not to English romanticism but to Dante and Shakespeare; and Leo Tolstoy, Henrik Ibsen, August Strindberg, and Richard Wagner meant far more to him in contemporary art than James Whitcomb Riley and Booth Tarkington. Far from urging feminine standards, he protested a merger between Radcliffe and Harvard because male students and faculty needed to continue the challenge of "masculine" competition in intellect. He accepted the existence of the ideal as a spiritual force that animates mere factual data, but he also called himself a pragmatist in a letter to William James whose book *Pragmatism* (1902) represents "the philosophy towards which I have blundered through my fifty years."[23]

If there was truth in Lowell's feeling that we must have a criticism before we have a literature, the explosion of creativity in the 1920s implies the existence of a great deal of antecedent criticism. In fact, however, the splintered, multifaceted state of American literary criticism at the turn of the century merely indicates something of the growing intellectual unrest which culminated in a second renaissance. Wendell's use of science, his evolutionary criticism, and his Taine-like attention to sociological factors place him in the camp of the literary democrats without their faith in progress or their confidence in democratic mediocrity. His attention to broader human characteristics than race, place, and time and his awareness of the European tradition locate him with George Woodberry, Brander Matthews, Irving Babbitt, and Paul Elmer More in the New Humanist group, though he himself clearly posits few universal standards of value. And his criticism, both impressionistic and analytic, recalls the work of Henry James and the objective-impressionists; but Wendell lacks the insight and the technical sense of James. That we may—though not with any ease—consider Wendell as either a tender-minded or a tough-minded critic, as either a despairing conservative or as a muted optimist, indicates the weakness, on one hand, of Wendell as a literary critic and his inability to transcend the conflcting crosscurrents of theory and opinion; but, on the other hand, our inability to categorize him reveals Wendell as a salient product of a confused time.

Van Wyck Brooks found two Bostons in the pre–World War I

days: one, the dying gasp of Brahmin Boston; the other, a milieu of
taste, culture, dissent that was soon to flower in the work of T. S.
Eliot. Wendell may be the epitome of the first group—the narrow
aristocrats looking to a dead past; but, as we shall see, Wendell had a
positive relationship with the other, more vital Boston in his correspondence with Amy Lowell. As we shall also see, the *Literary
History* demonstrates that his appreciation for the New England
past was not uncritical, and his belief in a Puritan dogmatism was
not at all personal. Wendell, in fact, is not unlike Brook's Epigoni
"in their revolt from democracy and realism, their desire to expunge
all remnants of the Puritan past."[24] And Wendell's admiration for
the British crown, his enthusiasm for the classics, his appreciation of
the hierarchic church parallels a famous royalist, classicist, Anglo-
Catholic of the 1930s, T. S. Eliot. As Brooks has written, "when
one added these tastes together, the royalism and the classicism,
the Anglo-Catholicism, the cults of Donne and Dante, the Sanskrit,
the Elizabethan dramatists and the French Symbolist poets, one
arrived at T. S. Eliot, the quintessence of Harvard. Together they
shaped his opposition to the 'cheerfulness, optimism and hopefulness' that stood for the point of view of great days of the past."[25]

We see Wendell's appreciation for Donne in his seventeenth-
century study; and his devotion to Dante, learned from Lowell, was
lifelong. Elizabethan drama was Wendell's continuing classroom as-
signment, and his interest in the French poets appeared as part of
the impetus behind Amy Lowell's book *Six French Poets*. When,
then, Warner Berthoff says that "the grounding of [Eliot's] thought
in polite opinion of the '80s and '90s is always worth noting,"[26] we must recognize Wendell's place in the Lowell-Eliot continuum. Indeed, remembering that Brooks, too, came out of that
same Harvard tradition, we might wonder whether Brooks, like
Ezra Pound in regard to Whitman, owes a debt to a teacher he
cannot easily admire.

Brooks maintained that Eliot reversed his country's tradition of
liberal democracy when he approved its "Tory, anti-democratic and
squirearchical character"; and the Wendell-Eliot association becomes real, if for no other reason, through Brooks's attack on them
both for the same reasons. Wendell's outlook on conditional and
highly contingent existence as the inherent quality of human despair
naturally derives from a temperament and a career which forever
presented a Prufrockian dichotomy between sterile actuality and

desire, and it parallels what in T. S. Eliot's 1922 poem so graphically appeared as one of the predominant themes of the early twentieth century. The "tradition" of spiritual unrest, skepticism, and sterility conveyed in the *Waste Land*, is transmitted from the last century not only by Henry Adams, William James, Hamlin Garland, E. A. Robinson but by Barrett Wendell as well.

Wendell's role as a teacher in this critical continuum between 1880 and 1920 is important. Herbert Howarth points out that T. S. Eliot fought against Charles W. Eliot's view that "good and sane men are liberal-minded" and that he did so "following the lead of two anti-presidential teachers: Babbitt and Wendell."[27] Moreover, when we read Wendell's words that "to know our place, as teachers of literature—or, at our highest as makers of it, or at least stimulators of others to make it—we must be aware of all those periods which have gone before us"; when we read, "our higher duty is not to neglect, but to select, and to reject—that is, so far as our focal business is cumulative. Then within our inmost selves must come the flash which can synthesize into new combination the rays of force from near and far, most needful of our radiant purpose,"[28] then we recall Eliot's "Tradition and the Individual Talent," in which he sees the force of tradition struck by the catalyst of imagination, the individual talent, into new art. Eliot writes, "It is part of the business of the critic to preserve tradition—where a good tradition exists. It is part of his business to see literature steadily and to see it whole . . . , to see the best work of our time and the best work of twenty-five hundred years ago with the same eyes."[29]

Wendell's gaze faltered as he looked about at the contemporary literary setting; but, as Howarth notes of Wendell, "There was an inner man who was no Tory; who had a hidden river of humanity, like Matthew Bramble's; who also saw facts clear." If he was not a man who could use tradition as a basis of comparison and analysis of literature, as he advocated and as both Pound and Eliot attempted, he did possess Eliot's first requisite of a critic—an interest in his subject matter and a talent for communicating an interest in it. Howarth claims that Eliot, when he wrote his 1929 essay on Dante, "essentially . . . was doing what Wendell and other Harvard teachers did: transmitting his enthusiasm to a new generation." It must be said that Wendell lacked the disciplined sensibility, the serious attention to formal principles of art, the analytical power, and the thoroughness and exactitude which the critic Eliot admired.

The mood and values which Wendell as a critic conveyed nevertheless contained more of a usable past than Brooks' generation admitted. And, despite the fact that Wendell "was fiery-frail, an actor, an exotic, an ape of Europe," he can be seen with Babbitt as an influence shaping T. S. Eliot "against the assumptions of his society." The influence is not wholly palpable, yet ours may be the question put by Howarth, "Did his example encourage Eliot on the way to the conservatism and royalism he was to acquire from the French?"[30]

Wendell stands close to the New Humanists when he expresses doubt about the romantic spirit of individual freedom, though in Emerson he sees the breaking of the old bonds of literary convention and a cultural upswing based on that same romantic theme. Yet, while his use of evolutionary principles would assume a more mature literary expression following that of the first American renaissance, he saw nothing in America like the new French literature of Balzac or Flaubert in their breaking of traditional shackles to present life as it is, or like Russian literature and Tolstoy, "certainly the greatest realist of modern literature," with "none of Zola's brutality and none of Howells' timidity."[31] It is then difficult to list Wendell with any mood of literary optimism at the end of the nineteenth century or to categorize him as one of the members of the American Academy of Arts and Sciences, who, one of the "last descendents of the great men of the 1850s . . . , still glowed with the evergreen optimism which had withered, almost at birth, from the young writers who had come of age and been destroyed in the nineties."[32] Critically his hopes were positive; between the scientifically accurate scholarship which was the "great glory of contemporary learning" and the "dilettante scholarship of tradition" there must be achieved some balance: "The scholars to come, then, who shall do the final work, have before them, I think, a task that neither the old scholarship nor the new has quite perceived or asserted. Before the final work can be done, the broad sympathy of the old school, discarding its fantastic vagaries, must unite with the cool sanity of the new. In every literary expression of the kind which shall by and by make a real comparative literature possible, there must be united in thorough fusion vitality and truth."[33] This vision, as we have seen it now in his life, his career, and his criticism is just as ambivalent and eclectic but more redemptive in his *Literary History*.

CHAPTER 5

National Inexperience

PERRY Miller has described turn-of-the-century attitudes toward American literature as "the serene persuasion that although the country had produced Irving, Emerson, Longfellow, it did not yet have a sufficient corpus to justify devoting so much as a manual to the record of its literature."[1] That John Macy's *Spirit of American Literature* (1913) marks the beginning of "real" American literary history is a commonplace today, as is the revolutionary impact of V. L. Parrington's *Main Currents in American Thought* (1930). And the products of that "revolution" have been prone to lump Charles F. Richardson's, Barrett Wendell's, and William P. Trent's work together as "the more orthodox literary histories" of genteel racism, aristocratic narrowness, and Anglo-Saxon prejudice. Only Moses Coit Tyler's work about the colonial period is considered an exception.

We may quickly summarize the official attitude toward Wendell, beginning with Van Wyck Brooks, who complained that American literature for Wendell meant "a minor and moribund branch" of England. *The Cambridge History of American Literature* claims that Wendell's *Literary History of America* is "essentially a history of the birth, the renaissance, and the decline of New England," and the *Literary History of the United States* finds Wendell so full of negative pronouncements that "the reader wonders why he wished to write the book at all."[2] William Dean Howells's "divided mind" over Wendell's history reveals the complexity of contradictory perspectives and attitudes toward this flawed but fascinating book: it is "an important work," wrote Howells; and, if Wendell had not produced "the best history of American literature, he had educated himself, in writing it, to produce some such history."[3]

While T. S. Eliot described Wendell's "monumental work" as "almost an admission, in a great many words, that there is no

93

American literature,"[4] the "almost" is important since there is a patriotism in Wendell's work which leads to his repeated assertion that, although the literature may be of slight aesthetic value, it radiates great historical value. Moreover, the *History* also demonstrates a critical honesty, for Wendell claims to acknowledge "no country but the Republic of letters." Inevitably, this honesty leads to a contradiction between the aristocratic Wendell, who detested Whitman's democratic euphoria, and the critical Wendell, who had to admire Whitman's evocative power. The essential complexity in the *History* of national inexperience opposed by real individual genius and craftsmanship is compounded by Wendell's political and social conservatism; by his sense of despair as the nineteenth century closed; and by his complicated, shifting viewpoints which reveal once more the frustrating and paradoxical ambiguities which plagued Wendell's career.

The book employs various structural devices that reflect the same multiplicity of critical viewpoints that we find in his other writing. Here these viewpoints form a series of referent frames, one within the other. The outermost frame unifies the book thematically: Wendell's conception of the American heritage of enthusiasm, versatility, and spontaneity from Elizabethan Puritans, which, because of the relaxed social pressures in the New World, produced the national characteristic, "inexperience." The next frame, with which Wendell structures this theme, is the same century-by-century organization found in *The Traditions of European Literature*. He divides American literature into seventeenth, eighteenth, and nineteenth centuries (not, significantly, including writers still living in 1900); and, at the beginning of each section, he compares the American literary scene with English literature of the same period. The third referent frame is still historical and comparative though more limited in scope; for, within each century division, Wendell compares regional literature: New York and Boston, the South and New England. Finally, the innermost concern of each section is the personal history of individual writers and, more particularly, Wendell's analysis of the artistic merit of these writers.

The weakness of Wendell's multiple-perspective framework derives from an inorganic unity, a unity achieved at times merely by juxtaposition. His organization by century arbitrarily marks the actual stages of national inexperience and hardly explains the significance of various regional productivity. The biographical facts of individual authors never work together with the larger theme of national inexperience; and, while the artistic merits of these writers coexist with the organization by century, with the comparisons to British literature, and at times even with the discussions of American experience, these merits do not appear as functions of the larger aspects of the *History*. In fact, the two inner frames—chronological and regional—seem to work apart from the outermost structure of national inexperience and the innermost structure of individual artistic ability. While these inner two frames are inseparable from Wendell's total effect, we must consider them first as subordinate to the interrelationship of individual artistry and the national character.

I *Chronology: England and America*

Wendell's division of American literature into centuries wherein he compares English with American writing evoked much contemporary notice and subsequent criticism, for in his comparative technique appears not only the attitude that earned him the reputation as an anglophile but the Boston prejudice which neglected southern and western writing in favor of the New England renaissance. Brander Matthews admired "the skill and success with which he has brought out and emphasized that our American literature is but a branch of English literature having its roots as firm in the glorious past and deriving as directly from Chaucer, Shakespeare, Milton and Dryden as does the other branch that flowers in Great Britain."[5]

T. S. Eliot, however, expressed the problem that the new literary historians had with Wendell: "Anyone who writes a history of American literature as *parallel* to Enlish or French literature, or any other literature . . . will be wrong, however moderate or just his claims for America may be. The justification for the history of American literature—instead of merely promoting the important Americans into a history of English literature—is that there is undoubtedly something American, and not English, about every American author."[6]

Certainly Wendell's prejudices stand out all too clearly. Part of the impulse behind his comparative method lies in its shock value—in what Wendell calls a "tonic for our complacency"—since "by the side of their English rivals the glories of our constellations do not shine so supremely bright as we let ourselves fancy when we

contemplated them alone" with a tendency to mutual admiration
and with the limited American experience which makes "New England overestimate itself" (445). Eliot's sense of Wendell's theme as
the nonexistence of American literature is clear when, asking what
New England has contributed to lasting literary expression, Wendell answers "not much" (445).

Predictably, then, his assessments of individual writers indicate
the similar literary production in England some half century before:
Timothy Dwight of the Connecticut Wits writes "Triumph of Fidelity" in the traditional manner of the early English eighteenth century, published in a year signalized in England by a collected edition of the poems of Robert Burns (123). Washington Irving's prose
reads much like that "which in England flourished most during the
mid years of the eighteenth century" (174), and William Cullen
Bryant displays a "formal sentimentality which had hardly characterized vital work in England for fifty years" (201). Wendell's comparisons create those easy generalizations that still figure in American literature textbooks: Brockden Brown is the American William
Godwin; Irving, the American Oliver Goldsmith; James Fenimore
Cooper, the American Sir Walter Scott; Bryant, the American
Wordsworth (228).

Wendell describes the American temper in two ways: his considered notion of American inexperience is sociological and environmental, and it stresses not just what America has added to English
literature but what is essentially American about that literature.
Even when he feels constrained to juxtapose Charles Dickens, William Thackeray, George Eliot, Alfred Tennyson, Thomas Carlyle,
and Matthew Arnold with Ralph Waldo Emerson, Walt Whitman,
Henry Wadsworth Longfellow, Oliver Wendell Holmes, and
Nathaniel Hawthorne, he summarizes the comparison by noting
that "you can hardly help feeling a difference, palpable even
though indistinct, undeniable even though hard to define" (528).
His distinctions just as often illustrate ones in kind as in merit.

Wendell's organization of American literature by century makes
clear his second approach to the American mind and that is
evolutionary. He stresses the inheritance of American literature
from the English past and eventually its difference from the past
because of a frontier environment. One of Wendell's characteristic
theses, as we see in his *Temper of the Seventeenth Century*, is the
fact of American character, which originated with early Elizabethan
settlers as spontaneous in temper, versatile in power, and enthusias-

tic in purpose (19, 27). As a generalization of Renaissance temper,
this idea is viable; but it hardly does justice to the distance that
separated the king's men from those Puritans who closed the theaters. Still, part of Wendell's concern is consciously to stress the
imaginative vitality of the Puritans—driven by the fervor of their
faith to view things not of this factual world but of another ideal
world—and not their well-known grimness. Cotton Mather especially in the *Magnalia* reveals the intensely imaginative American
Calvinist, writing with the spontaneous enthusiasm of the English
Elizabethans.[7]

English character evolved through war, regicide, and restoration
in the seventeenth century from that same Elizabethan fervor into
the solid, deliberate, conservative John Bull character (64). So,
then, while Wendell's conception of the English character originates
in Shakespeare's England and evolves through conflict with severe
social forces to produce a Doctor Johnson or a Charles Dickens, it
points out by contrast what the American temper is. With the relaxed social pressures of a frontier world, we understand why the
Elizabethan spirit of idealism and a love of individual freedom remains for Wendell fairly stable in America across three centuries.
We need to recall another of Wendell's ideal conceptions of this
country, as we see it in *Liberty, Union, and Democracy*, and that is
"our surprising power of assimilation." Through three centuries of
American life, "the absorptive power of the native human race remained undiminished, as indeed it still seems to remain" (70). The
temper of the English renaissance helped form this country; and,
due to the absence of traditional social pressures and the absorbing
quality of the new land, that temper continued strong in America
while it changed in England. Wendell's difficulty in subscribing to
the evolutionary principles of Spencer and his inability to accept the
democratic equality of Whitman's vision rests on this conservative
stance which asserts that America's strength is its homogeneity and
which fears that the increased heterogeneity at the end of the
nineteenth century means not social progress but dissolution of that
Anglo-Saxon strength by the hordes of immigrants which threaten
its "power of assimilation." To cite this flaw in Wendell's approach
to American literature—his failure to account seriously for particularly American pressures for change—is to take note of the historian
produced by an aristocratic Boston.

Wendell's prejudices enter clearly into his identification of divergent English and American characteristics, and that method governs

his comparison subsequently of American political, social, and literary facts and reveals even more his characteristically conservative views. The American Revolution grew out of the inexorable difference in national feeling. While the "glittering generalities" of the French philosophers appealed more emphatically than did English conservatism to the colonial energies of spontaneity, enthusiasm, and versatility, the abstract phrases of "radical" French thought appealed only superficially to Americans; for the underlying impulse of the American Revolution was the belief that "the rights for which men should die are not abstract but legal." Because the American Revolution was fought to maintain the rights inherited from England, it succeeded, whereas the French Revolution failed. Wendell, while revealing a pride in the tradition of Anglo-Saxon law and defending the war as a misunderstanding of both sides in efforts to assert legal rights of custom instead of the abstract "rights of man" (116), points to a problem still prevalent in the American mind, a problem that even conditions responses to Wendell himself—the split between the liberal words of democratic ideality and the pragmatism of conservative laws.

At the base of this political analysis lies the comparative method, and Wendell's feeling throughout the *Literary History* that, "without a constant sense of the influences which were alive in the New England air, the literature which finally arose there can hardly be understood ." His concern ultimately, of course, is literature, despite long chapters on English history and New England historians and scholars. In many respects his book is a study in the life of the American mind to 1900. And that life in the seventeenth and eighteenth centuries—while England produced its Milton and Dryden, Pope and Johnson—produced only one name, Cotton Mather, of any literary value, since the Elizabethan spontaneity, versatility, and enthusiasm were devoted to religious tracts; and only Jonathan Edwards and Benjamin Franklin achieved literary importance in the eighteenth century, a century more notable for its political concerns. These centuries Wendell values, nonetheless, for the evidence of a national character which came to first literary flower in nineteenth-century New York and Boston.

II *Regional Comparison*

This same Brahmin bias also reveals itself in his regional structuring when he compares New England and the South, whose idealism he appreciates if not its literature. In the first place, intellectual activity for Wendell actively distinguished New England from southern settlers "of the adventurous type which expresses itself far more in action than in words" (27). But, with regard to slavery, Wendell conservatively felt that the northern reform movement was "an unprecedented attack on that general right of property which the Common Law has always defended" (340); to Wendell, "an attack on slavery therefore involved a general attack on the whole basis of civilisation" (344).

With a note of regret Wendell states that the "better classes of Boston . . . have never forgotten that the ultimate dominance of the anti-slavery movement coincided with the final passing of political leadership . . . into the hands of another social class than that educated gentry" (352). Regardless of how he felt about the literature of this period, his social and political views erect a serious barrier to any objective appreciation. Harriet Beecher Stowe's *Old Town Folks* is better than *Uncle Tom's Cabin* despite the latter's "convincing power" and background (354). What marked the major North-South distinction in literature was the fact that in the North "there was no mob; the lower class in New England produced Whittier" (481), whereas southerners dissipated their energies in the "rigid maintenance of established order" threatened by "the risk of servile insurrection" (482).

The conclusions of Wendell's comparative method are expressed in his statement that "in the development of national character, even the North of America has lagged behind England; and the South has lagged behind the North." An Anglo-Saxon prejudice leads him to presuppose England as a standard and his racism determines his explanation of the lack of serious southern literature. Even his slighting of the West derives from his aristocratic belief that western immigration was composed mostly of "social degenerates" (502). We shall see, however, that in his view of American inexperience Wendell recognizes the greater literary potential of the South and West as opposed to that of a fading New England. His prejudices were real and serious; but they never wholly blinded him.

III   *National Inexperience*

While the frames of chronology and region obviously condition the structure and tone of the *Literary History*, the overriding theme of American inexperience, important as an interpretation of national consciousness, and the individual analysis of writers make the study

more significant than twentieth-century detractors have conceded.
As T. S. Eliot wrote in 1919, "It is inevitable that any work on
American literature should contain a good deal of stuffing. The fault
is not the lack of material so much as its lack of cohesion."[8] Wendell,
however, attempts to unify his history, to give cohesion to the literary movement of three centuries, by illustrating his thesis of "national inexperience." His Sorbonne lectures provide a definition for
that phrase which occurs throughout Wendell's commentaries on
American literature: "Variations in environment which alter national organisms I have grown accustomed to describe to myself by
the term national experience. By national inexperience, according-
ly, I mean at once the absence of such altering and distorting environment, and a certain relaxation of external pressure, which pre-
vents fixity of habit; this is evident even in individual American
life."[9]

Such experience exists "only under conditions where the pressure
of external fact, social, political, and economic, is relaxed,—under
conditions, in short, where the individual type is for a while
stronger than environment" (33). This relaxed social pressure, along
with the American power to absorb immigrants, maintained as vital
much of the Elizabethan and Puritan vigor while the Civil War and
Protectorate in England destroyed the youthful exuberance of the
Renaissance (25). National inexperience one way means "social
stagnation," but, as he writes in *Stelligeri*, it "does not mean, of
course, that human life has not existed here in all its real complexity. It means that hitherto our communities have generally
been so far from overcrowded, and our people so free to make their
way wither they would and could, that in America the material
problems of life have presented themselves less regularly than in
Europe" (11–12).

When Wendell talks about materiality, about what he feels to be
an instinctual disregard for fact, we must be careful not to dismiss
this as merely a Puritan ideality. Wendell's term means neither a
retreat from experience nor a negative attitude toward it. Nor does
his inexperience denote *no* experience, but rather a particular kind
of felt relation to the New World; it is a positive relationship, albeit a
thin one, in which the pressures of society are reduced from societal
problems to the basic human ones of mere existence in which the
social man counts far less than the simple, separate person. He
writes in 1903: "Though the material and economic conditions of
early New England were hard and narrow, they were remarkably

simple, and free from every kind of social complexity. The very sparseness of population made the struggle for life chiefly a contest with the forces of nature."[10]

Wendell's sense of the Puritan is far less the denial of the facts of human existence generally associated with American Victorians than an affirmation of the imaginative fervor and idealism that brought the early settlers to the New World. His concept of inexperience closely parallels the popular thesis in American literature of innocence and the New Adam. Puritan "total depravity" Wendell equates with the Darwinian principle of the "struggle for existence," but the relaxation of social pressure in the New World created a rather marked contrast to the "dense, wicked old world, whose passion ran high and deep," with its "vices and crimes, big as its brave old virtue" (16–17). The New World "inexperience" could not support the old idea of depravity; therefore, greater stress came to be placed on the Puritan doctrine of election, which is for Wendell, as we have observed, a religious view synonymous with the Spencerian notion of the survival of the fittest.

Given the relative absence of social pressures in America, the imaginative impulse of Puritanism, and the necessity of human survival in a frontier existence, the steps from Cotton Mather to Walt Whitman and Horatio Alger were inevitable. As Calvinism faded, pragmatism rose; and the self-made man replaced the concept of God's elect. As faith receded, imaginative energy was refocused and, evolving through Unitarianism, became the American brand of romanticism, transcendentalism.

Wendell's attitude that social density carries with it a greater sense of evil seems like the romantic concept of evil as a function of man's institutions. But Wendell is no romantic; rather, he feels transcendental philosophy's liberal, optimistic concept of the nature of man to be extremely myopic. Furthermore, the extreme individualism of the movement harmfully denigrated an appreciation for artistic craft. If Wendell believed that American literature in the middle of the nineteenth century had produced few great artists, his belief derives from the idea that great art arises from the apprehension of tension between good and evil—the Everlasting Yay and the Everlasting Nay—not from a shallow world of merely personal, as opposed to social, experience. In any case, Wendell repeatedly finds his theory an illuminating one in nearly all his works to explain the American mind and the growth of American letters.

Lewis Gates called this theory the "radical part" of Wendell's study, but he noted that it also served to "make his interpretation of literature a very genuine and suggestive criticism of life."[11] We have seen how Wendell developed his thesis of election to support an aristocratic faith in political and social order; and, in the more general cultural development traced in the *Literary History*, the conservative tone similarly dominates. When he looks at eighteenth-century literature for an example of the American character, he compares a passage from Francis Hopkinson that analyzes the commonsense strength of the average Englishman and American with Crèvecoeur's famous passage on "this new man"; and he finds Hopkinson's American to be "afterall, a human being; Crèvecoeur's American is no more human than some ideal savage of Voltaire" (115). There is an essential difference between the view of an American Adam come to the new garden to attempt anew the construction of God's City on the Hill and Wendell's position that, confronted by a wilderness world, the enthusiastic, spontaneous, and versatile Elizabethan Puritan was apt not to think of the New World as a new start but to believe Calvin mistaken about the extreme depravity of man. The results in one way come to the same thing—a view of American innocence and optimism; and in both lie the seeds of tragedy: the American innocent must inevitably become experienced—man must fall—and the inexperienced in a sparsely settled frontier must eventually build a dense society in which all man's depravity would once more be played out. The inevitability of the pattern could, of course, be traced in the naturalistic impulse of his own day, and characteristically Wendell did not know whether to lament the passing of an innocent if flawed craftsmanship or to celebrate the arrival of experienced and bleak artistry.

The ideals of the young society free of older social ills were expressed in that first century when American Puritans asserted the need for man to exert his will in concert with God's will (53); and the literature it produced, like the poetry of Anne Bradstreet, reflected merely the provincial maintenance of older Elizabethan traits and manners (56). But the eighteenth century witnessed an increasing divergence from the older theology of sin and grace depicted in the eloquent orthodoxy of Jonathan Edwards and the new practical ethics of Benjamin Franklin; and this divergence occurred in a world "so relieved from the pressures of external fact that people generally behaved much better than is usual in earthly history" (89). Election in the eighteenth century became a pragmatic business:

"such commonsense as Franklin's ultimately makes human beings behave in a manner so far from superficially damnable that you might be at pains to distinguish them from God's own elect" (100).

While there is logic in Wendell's theory of relaxed social conditions, we cannot help but feel a certain naiveté that almost shrouds the past in a view of ideality. In many ways, the social innocence that Wendell posits for the seventeenth and eighteenth century is nonsense and fails to account seriously for the social realities of colonial Boston, New York, and Philadelphia. In so far as he finds that Franklin's business sense makes him sound like a proto-Horatio Alger, Wendell's views reflect a genteel tendency to defend the "theological" view of big business; but his claim that the "highest development of intellectual life in New England coincided with its greatest material prosperity" (245) is no argument for the captains of industry. Instead, it offers insight into Wendell's evolutionary theory of American literary development. Great art does not proceed without a real sense of the tragic in human life, without the opposition of experience to innocence; nor does it, for Wendell, develop without the strength behind it of a unified tradition. The South possessed the greatest strength of solid English tradition, but it also had the greatest cultural simplicity. New York showed greater signs of developing a density of institutional and materialistic experience, but it had as yet produced little art because of a larger, more heterogeneous population and thus a lack of central ideas and tradition. But Boston, on the other hand, had the tradition; and by the early 1840s it had also the accumulated social experience to produce the first great period in American art.

It is clear that Wendell might be accused of provinciality since he admits that New York already shared more with old London and Paris "than with ancestral America" (452). He is also clearly an anglophile in his appreciation of the English Puritan tradition that helped give force to the New England renaissance. But, at the same time, we see reflected here the same critical, evolutionary theory with which he structures the earlier study of Shakespeare and his subsequent book on seventeenth-century literature. The cyclical rise and fall of literature begins with intense, if flawed, imaginative fervor—revealed in the Renaissance by the drama of Marlowe—and fades when the factual or real, material world overcomes the imaginative—characterized by Webster, Ford, and Middleton. The high points in literary history for Wendell have always been those

periods when imaginative energy and factual experience coalesce, as
they did most powerfully in William Shakespeare. Boston in the
1840s *almost* represents just such a period.

The early literary movements of the nineteenth century in
Hartford; the New York literature of Irving, Cooper, and Bryant;
and the literature of the South were all foreshortened because they
"still lacked national experience ripe for expression" in a form that
would be distinctive (103, 184, 499). Inexorably, however, American experience was accumulating, primarily in New England, where
it led to a "Renaissance."[12] Wendell's chapters on this literary
movement, especially those on Unitarianism and transcendentalism, display a marked change of tone, of style, of attitude; he
appears for the while to have forgotten about England. The enthusiasm with which he describes the effects of national inexperience, tempered by the intellectual and social forces of the early
eighteenth century, to explain the positive qualities of the period
reveals a deep appreciation of the literature of midcentury Boston.
The intellectual activities of George Ticknor, Jared Sparks, William
Ellery Channing, and Edward Everett which predate the best work
of Emerson, Longfellow, and Hawthorne evoke the days when
Thomas Linacre and William Grocyn were reviving letters at Oxford
in another century.

Wendell treats the development of Unitarianism and subsequently transcendentalism as the natural outgrowth of Puritan
ideals situated in the frontier environment of relaxed social forces.
He is fully aware of the role played by English and European
romantics: "No two men of letters in the nineteenth century affected
English thought more evidently than Coleridge and Carlyle" (296),
and by 1840 in Boston few educated people "could not talk with glib
delight about German philosophy, German literature, and German
music." He points out, too, the influence on trancendentalism of
French eclectic philosophers like Victor Cousin and Théodore Jouf-
froy, whose names "were as familiar to Yankee ears as were those of
Locke, Descartes or Kant" (296); but Wendell sees a single thread of
continuity tying Puritan, Unitarian, and transcendentalist to the
same national character: "The New Englanders of our Renaissance
were no longer Puritans; they had discarded the grim dogmas of
Calvinism; but so far as Puritanism was a lifelong effort to recognise
and to follow ideals which can never be apprehended by unaided
human senses, they were still Puritan at heart" (372).

It was no wonder, says Wendell, that an innocent, youthful soci-

ety which argued for the fact of innate human good would turn from
a theology born in Augustine's "decadent" Roman Empire and in
Calvin's "pervasively wicked" Europe (278–79). By the time of
Jonathan Edwards, "Calvinistic dogma and national inexperience
were unwittingly at odds" (280). Although Wendell could easily
have cited the influence of Lockean philosophy on the Unitarian
movement, his concern is to stress the essential American quality.
The national inexperience of America by 1805 needed Christ "not as
a redeemer, but as an example," and Channing enunciated the
full meaning of Unitarian thought, which emphasizes the goodness
of man—made in God's image—who needs to follow that light given
most clearly by God in Christ (285).

The romantic revolution occurred around the same period of the
ascendency of Unitarianism; and, while we might simplistically find
that the romanticism in New England in the 1830s, 1840s, and 1850s
imitated several decades later the literary impulse of England and
Europe, "the revolutionary spirit showed itself more plainly" in
Unitarianism (291), an earlier phase of the American romantic
movement that later produced in Emerson one of the most
characteristic expressions of American thought, with "a note as fresh
as was the most extravagant revolutionary expression in Europe"
(291). Wendell explicitly sums up the movement of American
thought in the early nineteenth century: "To say that Unitarianism
caused the subsequent manifestation of free thought in New England would be too much; but no one can doubt that the world-wide
revolutionary spirit, of which the first New England manifestation
was the religious revolution effected by Unitarianism, impelled the
following generation to that outbreak of intellectual and spiritual
anarchy which is generally called Transcendentalism" (292).

Wendell recalls Kant when he defines the knowable, empirical
world and the other world of "undemonstrable truths which must
always transcend human experience" (293). But, while alluding to
the influence of the German idealists, Wendell finds that the tran-
scendentalists intellectually and emotionally "followed an instinct
innate in their race. They were descended from two centuries of
Puritanism; and though the Puritans exerted their philosophical
thought within dogmatically fixed limits, they were intense idealists
too. Their whole temperamental energy was concentrated in efforts
definitely to perceive absolute truths quite beyond the range of any
earthly senses" (293–94).

Wendell's chronological progress through American literature carries him only to 1860 and American romanticism. His concepts of the American heritage from Puritanism, his phrase "national inexperience" to describe the American mind, and his critical theories about the nature of literary art reveal a characteristically conflicting set of biases. His English sensibilities assert the importance of the Anglo-Saxon heritage; his New England Brahminism is fervent in his praise of the Boston culture; and his Americanism approves the "devout free thought" of Emerson's philosophy, while his Tory prejudice fears the concomitant loss of order. And his sense of artistic merit is not convinced about the excellence of American literature by the 1860s.

IV *Art and Reality*

Wendell shares the opinion of many later critics as to the effects of this national inexperience. On one hand its value is clear: when, for two hundred years, the intellectual tyranny of English forms and Puritan tenets had kept the native mind cramped within the limits of tradition, Emerson fearlessly stood forth as the chief representative of that movement which asserted the right of every individual "to think, to feel, to speak, to act for himself, confident that so far as each acts in sincerity good shall ensue" (327). But that same innocent vigor was also its weakness. Like Henry James's view earlier in his famous Hawthorne essay, Wendell's view is also the same one expressed later by T. S. Eliot: "Their world was thin; it was not corrupt enough." Emerson in his attempt to express truth, "just as in his whole knowledge of life . . . was limited by the national inexperience" (327); and Thoreau's work "is always tinctured with his own disturbing individuality" (336). Limited experience combined with Whittier's "lack of humor to make his writings superficially commonplace" (360), and Hawthorne lived for almost fifty years confined by "isolated, aesthetically starved New England" (428).

Their world was shallow, their taste untutored, and part of the American renaissance lies in its "spontaneous enthusiasm," an unfeigned eagerness with all the "fervor of a race which had been aesthetically starved" (297–98). For Wendell, all this enthusiasm coexisted with a "guileless confusion of values" (298). As he describes the nature and weakness of American art to his own day he finds romanticism its enabling clause psychologically and its failure aesthetically. Theoretically, the conditions in New England were right for artistic success; but, in reality, that literature still mirrored more idealism and innocence than imagination, craft, or experience. Its writers, with a few exceptions, as we shall see in the next chapter, still did not know enough. Americans in New England had found their young Spenser, their Marlowe, but they still awaited their Shakespeare—the genius who for critics in the twentieth century is probably Wendell's contemporary and acquaintance Henry James. American literature to the beginning of Wendell's own career then proved essentially to be shallow in content and controlled, if imitative, in form.

Wendell's attitude toward form is an interesting, but a somewhat eccentric explanation of cause and effect. Since Irving, the short story has represented the most characteristic American art form for economic reasons—"short stories have usually been more profitable to writers and more convenient to editors than long novels" (516)— and for, of all things, reasons of conscience—compared to the English novel and its "disregard for form unprecedented in other civilized literature," short stories "most generally have complete and finished form," and the American conscience, "always a bit overdeveloped" has provided impetus in American literary craft, since "no one who lacks artistic conscience can write an effective short story" (177). This statement involves Wendell's Puritan predilections; if the superlative form he discerns in American literature is not an escape from the more realistic facts of life, it is a way of compensating for the lack of the harsher realities of life in a society where social evils are supposedly few or nonexistent.

Wendell's stance offers no support to the charge that American Victorians failed to recognize any other human realm than the abstract or idealistic as a source for American authors. Wendell concluded, as does Richard Chase in his study of the American novel, that the literature resulting from national inexperience is the romance "whose motive is mysterious" (168); "the darkly passionate idealism of the Puritans had involved a tendency towards conceptions, which when they reached artistic form must be romantic" (432).

Perhaps this attitude echoes an American fear of experience which anti-Puritan critics and artists of this century inveighed against, but it also represents the continued fascination in American literature and criticism with the dichotomy between "good" and "evil," between innocence and awareness. Wendell set out to ascertain the temper of American literature and to elucidate its sources.

His own perspective prevented him from labeling that temper a fear of experience, though that psychologically may be the case; neither, however, could his critical honesty allow him to admire inexperience merely because it existed. Wendell and Howells in fact clashed over the degree of excellence they found in American letters. Whereas Howells praised the cleanly American characteristics in literature, Wendell believed American inexperience, New England idealism, and conscientious concern for form may explain our national literature; such conditons may produce work "in every aspect . . . sincere and pure and sweet," but beauty of spirit cannot cover the fact that American expression is "lacking in scope, in greatness" (446).

Wendell's dilemma is explicit and may well explain his reticence to discuss contemporary literature; for, while he admires temperamentally the absence of the "pruriently foul . . . germ-like suggestions prominent in European literature," he recognizes professionally the impossibility of literature to exist in a vacuum apart from such complex social tensions. Aesthetically, the best art knows the tragic qualities of human life, qualities hitherto missing from American experience (we must remember that Wendell like most of his contemporaries failed to recognize Melville's significance). Emotionally and politically, Wendell was a tough-minded evolutionist; he despaired over the dissolution of the "central" American heritage of New England into the chaotic, ethnological, and sectional hodgepodge of the modern United States. Artistically, on the other hand, his language is theological rather than evolutionary; therefore, the mechanical dissipation of energy becomes the fall from innocence into experience, and the new dispensation, the chaos of modern experience, may provide the stuff great art is made of. With this perspective, then, we may better understand Wendell's uncertainty as he faced a new century marked by increasing social experience, an increasingly heterogeneous population, and complicated ethical and moral situations as to whether the new literature meant a dawn or a sunset. He often refused to say so explicitly, but his theory predicts, correctly, a dawn.

Wendell seems often to epitomize the American "boy-man," a perfect Jamesian character isolated by the heritage and conditioning of inexperienced New England, yet longing too for the experience of Europe. There is little justice in Brooks's complaint that national inexperience was "the standard that lurked in the depths of [Wendell's] mind. The real experience of the country, which found a voice in literature, was vague and repugnant to Wendell; and naturally he was half-hearted, therefore, even about its greatest writers."[13] The truth seems that his own experience in New England limited his vision to an honest belief that innocence really, though narrowly, characterized American literature. Experience was a medium in European literature, and Henry James made it his great subject. Wendell feared no loss of purity, no loss of naive innocence; indeed, like James, Wendell had long admired European society and its literature. What he feared most was the loss of homogeneous strength and order—the New England order to which he clung defensively. He nonetheless saw the artistic necessity, while fearing its inevitability, of the break from the Brahmin past; but it would take Brooks's generation finally to effect that break. For the James figure as historian, the way out of inexperience is back toward the kind of European experience from which the American settler had originally departed. That experience in 1900 was more and more to be found right in Irish Boston, and Wendell turned alternately East and West. He honestly could not decide whether the new America was good or bad.

CHAPTER 6

Biography and Art

NATIONAL inexperience thematically structures Wendell's comparative method and his aristocratic respect for New England writers, but in *A Literary History of America* Wendell is finally concerned with "pure letters." Nowhere else is the characteristic Wendell ambivalence so clear. The kind of social distinction Wendell is so obviously aware of—Whittier's coming from "sound country stock," Cooper's father as "something like a feudal lord," Longfellow "as the son of a lawyer in the palmiest days of the New England bar," and Whitman as the son of a Brooklyn carpenter and builder—matter very little in his final analysis of the literature. Those writers whose class he should approve—Holmes, Longfellow, Lowell—are the men whose writing little impresses him; and the writers whose class most disturbed his Brahmin sensibilities—Whitman and Poe—are the men whose writing he values most.

The pressures of Wendell's temperament, his heritage, and his time led him chauvinistically to promote much that was important only to aristocratic Boston. That stance—during a tumultuous *fin de siècle* era—we can understand. But there is also in the *Literary History* a critic whose intellectual honesty leads him to assess individual writers apart from their class, the critic who struggles to free himself from provincial blindness to assert the real artistry he discerned in American literature. For example, Wendell remarks that the "unedifying question" of Poe's life, his "inferior" social class, "need not seriously concern us" because his work "will always enrich the literature of the language in which it was written."[1] And Whitman, despite his life with "those half-criminal wanderers whom we now call tramps," has the "paradoxical merit of eminence" (465, 469). And the chronology of Hawthorne's life "becomes accidental . . . , for above all the rest . . . he was an artist" (427).

Like so many of the younger generation after the Civil War,

Wendell was aware of the popular and physical presence of many of those men of the 1840s who lived so long into the century, and he, too, took a certain pride in their work though he could hardly muster real admiration for their entire corpus. Howells felt that "Professor Wendell's radical disqualifications for his work seem absence of sympathy for his subject." The case more appropriately appears to have been that the conflict of his real sympathy—obvious from a lifelong attention to American literature in classes and books—with his critical integrity forced him to rank many of those beloved old names like Bryant, Longfellow, and Whittier lower than Howells could accept. Wendell seemed aware of the duality of his vision; for he said, after him "posterity will judge. . . . It will judge, too, with unthinking impartiality—without acrimony, without tenderness."[2]

I *Before the "Renaissance"*

Wendell's vacillating stance emerges early in his treatment of Philip Freneau, whose material and poetic ability are wholly new in such poems as the "Indian Burying Ground," which is marked by the "true beauty" of "genuineness and simplicity" (133); but, when Wendell remembers Keats, he is constrained to add: "taken by itself, 'The Indian Burying Ground' may fairly excite our patriotic enthusiasm to an excessive degree; a comparison with the 'Grecian Urn' may recall our patriotism to the limits of common-sense" (134). Similarly, he swings back and forth about Brockden Brown between calling him "imitative" and admiring his "instinctive sense of formal phrasing" (166). In Irving, Wendell finds a characteristic trait of American humor (which for Wendell is continuous from Franklin to Mark Twain) in his blending of fact, exaggeration, and extravagance; but his "style, meanwhile, is rather like that of Goldsmith" (173). He accurately describes Irving as the first master of the short story, maintaining that "the artistic conscience revealed in the finish of Irving's style and his mastery of the short story . . . may be called characteristic of his country." But we are left finally to choose between the Irving of "admirable and persistent sense of form," of "delicate, refined classic style," and the man "animated by no profound sense of the mystery of existence" (179).

How, too, are we to feel about Cooper when we first read that he "must have written with careless haste," with "little . . . tack in the matter of style," and then hear that, despite his "clumsiness and prolixity," he is "well worth reading" (183–84)? Wendell here dismisses his English standard, for to compare Cooper with Scott is needlessly to belittle Cooper; rather, the American novelist demonstrates the American inexperience. Wendell notes that Cooper was hampered by "a slighter, less varied, less human past than that of Scott's England or Scotland" (184–85). As he contrasts the abstract, idealistic quality of Cooper's characters placed in very real American settings, Wendell puts his finger on a major quality of American romance, though after all he must conclude that "neither Brown, nor Irving, nor Cooper has left us anything profoundly significant." And William Cullen Bryant is a poet, as Lowell indicated earlier, of simplicity, of "luminosity," with a thematic relevance and serious craftsmanship; yet his artistry is undercut by a dispassionate coolness and by "a somewhat formal sentimentality which had hardly characterized vital work in England for fifty years" (200–1).

The question we need to raise here is whether Wendell's attitude, which ends so ambivalently, derives from an inability to accept the basic aspects of the American life depicted by these writers, from a Bostonian belief that the New York writers achieved less than the writers of New England's renaissance, from an unfortunate overawareness of contemporary English literature, or from a narrow class view that denied the initial quality of the writers themselves. All these positions, raised against him with some justice by critics in this century, are real; but, struggling from beneath the weight of all these biases, a tentative critical voice finds merit in all of these writers. But the real difficulty Wendell feels about being more positive is the actual quality of the writers he discusses. Ironically the very thing that obstructs his ability to appreciate the democratic Whitman is the impulse he misses in earlier authors: "In its beginning American literature of the nineteenth century was marked rather by delicacy than by strength, by palpable consciousness of personal distinction rather than by any outburst of previously unphrased emotion as on general principles democracy might have been expected to excite" (203).

II *New England Renaissance*

Wendell discovers more of the vitality he sought in the New England renaissance, but the discovery still bares the scars of his ambiguity. Emerson's distinction results from his individualism and his "serene insolence." "Nature" is beautiful, serene, obscure, stimulating, permeated with the idealism which was the basis of his philosophy. Wendell underlines Emerson's idealism as well as his

modern and human expression, "perennial as that of Scripture itself"
(316). Wendell voices, too, what still remains something of a critical
commonplace, that Emerson's "astonishing lack of method is familiar," but he rightly points out at the same time the sermon structure
in Emerson's essays (317). Emerson's unsystematic philosophy
comprises both the ideal realm of the unknowable, transcendental
"spiritual laws" and the practical world. Though Wendell dislikes
Emerson's poetry for its "erratic oddity of form," he nevertheless
evaluates Emerson without his usual equivocation. Given the omission of Emily Dickinson from Wendell's *History* and his difficulty in
accepting Whitman, it is not surprising that Wendell missed one of
Emerson's major influential qualities. Such a flaw, perhaps, indicates something of Wendell's narrow vision toward his subject, but
he still recognized Emerson ultimately as the "living prophet" of
American ideal individualism (327). Wendell sees Emerson's work
as essentially American; still, in 1900, quite modern; and as "lasting-
ly human" as Dante and Shakespeare.

Another example of Wendell's narrow enthusiasm for the Concord writers is his classification of Thoreau as one of "the lesser men
of Concord." Wendell's bias against radical French thought underlies his observation that Thoreau reasons out the individualism
which Emerson balances with practicality "to its logical extremes"
with a revolutionary revulsion against civilized artificiality.
Thoreau's sympathy for nature, Wendell feels, almost precludes real
sympathy for human nature and is "often so assertive as to repel a
sympathy which it happens not instantly to attract" (334). This fact,
plus the distinction between Thoreau the farmer's son and Emerson
the son of traditional aristocracy, seems to bar Thoreau from the
upper ranks of American artists; for, while *Walden's* structure "falls
to pieces," Thoreau "was in his own way a literary artist of unusual
merit" (332); he evidenced much greater power in constructing a
sensitive, rhythmical prose. His work is forever colored by an unhealthy egotism, but his passionate feeling for nature gives him
"lasting Power." Once more Wendell's evaluation lies between a
positive assessment of Thoreau's artistry, his "loving precision of
touch," and the negative pressure of Wendell's philosophical and
social prejudice. "Thoreau was a more conscientious artist than
Emerson, [but the] constant obtrusion of his personality ranges him
in a lower rank" (337).

Similarly, the very fact of their ephemeral popularity provides
Wendell with grounds for faulting Longfellow and Whittier (364,

386). A simple, "dignified passion" and an "impregnable simplicity" are all that allow Wendell to feel that Whittier "may remain for posterity a living poet," but not even those traits elevate Whittier beyond the level of commonplace sentiment (364). Moreover, Wendell cannot decide whether Longfellow's "Psalm of Life" is "utter simplicity or reminiscent triteness." Even though Longfellow's poetry evinces clarity of phrase, and "delicacy of rhythm," it hardly approaches the richer wisdom he could have found in European literature. Yet bold would be the critic, exclaims Wendell, who would not accept the view of Longfellow's greatness, at the same time that he concludes with obvious equivocation: "He was never passionate; neither in his life nor in his verse does he ever seem to have been swept away by feeling. On the other hand . . . his taste was unerring, and his sentiment gently sympathetic. His real office was to open the flood-gates of that modern [European] literature in whose flashing beauty he delighted, and whose murky depths he never quite suspected" (390).

In Wendell's discussion of James Russell Lowell and Oliver Wendell Holmes we find the most pronounced imbalance between slight critical observation and lengthy commentary on their lives, their careers, and their relationship to the whole cultural environment that came to flower in midcentury New England. Wendell admires his former teacher Lowell for his "serious critical spirit . . . , Yankee good sense, and . . . surprising facility of idiomatic phrase" in the "Fable for Critics" and in the "Biglow Papers," but he dismisses *Sir Launfal* for the "amateurishly extravagant whimsicality and pedantry" which hampered Lowell's whole career (400). And Holmes is the shrewd, swift, volatile master of witty social verse whom Wendell absurdly compares to Voltaire and whose work really recalls the English spirit of the eighteenth century (416). Wendell's major interest is to demonstrate their fusion of the humanities with humanity, their leadership if not their literature, in a time when "the old formal traditions had been broken; our native mind had been enfranchised; and people were searching the eternities for vistas of truth and beauty which had been obscured by the austere dogma of the Puritans" (416).

III   *Less Ambivalence, Greater Art*

There are serious faults of omission in this list of writers (Melville and Dickinson most strikingly), faults of critical generalities and of narrow perspective in Wendell's feelings toward these writers. We cannot overlook these flaws, nor can we wonder that a younger generation in the twentieth century, searching as vigorously for a usable past as young writers in the 1830s sought a purely American art, would find Wendell's equivocations unpalatable. Still, we need to recall that Melville, Dickinson, and Whitman waited till the 1930s and 1940s for popular and critical attention. Moreover, Wendell's wavering emerges not only from his own personal uncertainty but from his critical inability to affirm the old literary giants. Even today critical opinion has not, with the exception of Thoreau and Emerson, elevated these writers much above Wendell's negative evaluations. That his criticism is more than the accident of Anglo-Saxon and Brahmin prejudice appears all the more certain when we look at his judgments of three writers that modern criticism still considers important nineteenth-century American artists—Poe, Hawthorne, and Whitman—for these writers evoke all of Wendell's prejudice and force his critical integrity to struggle all the harder in order to assert their artistic value.

The general content of his views toward these three writers is not necessarily unique. We can hardly praise him for an increasingly positive attitude toward Poe, for instance, since, despite a tentative appreciation of the Virginia poet and author whom Howells could not accept, that shifting perspective parallels the general critical shift in judgments from George E. Woodberry's study in 1885 to his revised version of that work in the Poe centenary year, 1909. Hawthorne had long been a New England favorite, and Wendell's view of his provincialism postdates James's famous study. Even in the case of Whitman, such a genteel writer as Edmund Clarence Stedman had managed as early as the 1880s to evince enthusiasm for the Good Grey Poet. The value lies in the fact that, despite its infamous negativity, we find such positive criticism on the more important authors discussed. These criticisms show, furthermore, the Boston historian's attempt to balance honesty and prejudice and the Brahmin's awareness that a safe old New England was dead. Beneath the aristocratic stance, there is the honest critic whose approach to "pure" American letters rests on the realization that for American writers "to give their expression resemblance of reality they had no medieval relics to guide them, no enduring local traditions, thick and strong about them. They were compelled to rely on sheer force of creative imagination."[3]

IV *Hawthorne*

Wendell's attitude toward Hawthorne shows little of his usual equivocating. Solitary and imaginative, Hawthorne not only expresses his "meanings in words of which the beauty seems sure to grow with the years" but articulates the "inalienable emotional heritage of Puritanism." Summarizing the roles of writers in the New England renaissance, Wendell designates Emerson as its prophet; Whittier, its reformer; Longfellow, its academic poet; Lowell, its humanist; and Holmes, its rationalist. Hawthorne stands above these as eminently its artist, "an artist, who lived for nearly fifty years only in his native country, daily stirred to attempt expression of what our Yankee life meant. Of all our men of letters he was the most indigenous; of all, the least imitative" (430). He was gifted with a "pervasive sense of form" and with the romantic temperament so typically native in America and traceable to "the darkly passionate idealism of the Puritans," whose sense of depravity and eternal retribution always haunted Hawthorne. Wendell admired the classical tradition and Puritanism because both understood life to include the light and dark forces of life. For Wendell, Hawthorne's work transcends the narrowness of romanticism not only by its craft but by its subject matter. In his solitary nature, his sense of the mysteries of life and sin, and his self-searching instinct, Hawthorne reflects the essential Puritan spirit, not only in its imaginative drive but in its recognition of the sense of human tragedy.

And Wendell finds Hawthorne essentially American in his self-conscious awareness of form; "starved of antiquity," living in "isolated, aesthetically starved New England," Hawthorne for Wendell, as for Poe, combines classical precision of form and artistic craftsmanship with a limited vision to express with beauty the facts and the sense of mystery that lie beyond physical human life. Wendell even becomes philosophical to explicate this combination of Puritan consciousness and aesthetic form: "though artistic conscience be very different from moral, the two have an aspiration toward beauty." The Aquinean concept of ethics and aesthetics underlies Wendell's appreciation of Hawthorne's artistic concern with "beauty of conduct" and "beauty of expression" (433). There is shadow about the formal substance of this romantic sentiment, however; "one grows aware . . . of its unmistakable rusticity; in terms of thought as well as phrase one feels monotony, provincialism, a certain thinness"—attributable to the isolated quality of Hawthorne's and of American life.

T. S. Eliot remarked that "the great figures of American literature are peculiarly isolated, and their isolation is an element, if not of their greatness, certainly of their originality." Perhaps the only prejudice implicit in this chapter is Wendell's humanistic tendency that would assert great literary potential where life is denser if more corrupt. But as T. S. Eliot noted further, "Barrett Wendell's 'Literary History of America' remains the best reference"[4] for the indigenous strength in American isolation; for Hawthorne's merit proves to be characteristic of provincial, inexperienced New England whose ideals, heritage, habit of conscious form, and awareness of mystery and sin "impelled him constantly to realize in his work those forms of beauty which should most beautifully embody the ideals of his incessantly creative imagination," to express "the deepest temper of that New England race which brought him forth" (434–35). Wendell sees finally in Hawthorne the artist who combined a heightened sensitivity to life with masterful expression.

V *Poe*

In Wendell's first book on American literature, *Stelligeri* (1893), he uses the words "fantastic and meretricious," "falsity," "sham," "wild," and "freakish" to illustrate his feelings toward Edgar Allan Poe (138–39). By 1900, however, he can in the *Literary History* speak of Poe's haunted imagination as "handled with something like mastery" (163). Despite the fact that Wendell sees Poe as on outsider and a Bohemian, he points out that Poe's fantastic European reputation obscures the "doubtful repute" of his life. Wendell believes Poe's criticism to be largely journalistic, though at the same time brave and sincere and on writers like Tennyson and Mrs. Browning excellent. Poe's philosophical writing, which makes Wendell rightly "suspicious," grows from its "intense ingenuity and unlimited scholarly ignorance" (211). His poetry tends to the unrealistic and the excessive. Yet "from beginning to end his temper had the inextricable combination of meretriciousness and sincerity" (213). If much of Poe's writing reveals grotesque fantasy, it nevertheless reveals as well the "melodramatic creature of genius" (214). Wendell's usual double vision explains Poe's European popularity by the decadent quality of his work (never really specified) but

locates him in the American setting through his "singular clean-
ness," his "instinctive purity." It is difficult to understand J. B.
Hubbell's belief that Wendell had difficulty fitting Poe into the
American tradition[5] because for Wendell Poe's "rare sense of form,"
his strenuous "artistic conscience," is a "trait more characteristic
of America than of England" (217).

The flaws Wendell discovers in Poe's work are staginess, un-
necessarily ornamental verse, morbidity, and "lack of spiritual insight." Wendell is put off by Poe's inferior social position and by his
southern origins; yet he explicitly cites his Americanness as a function of the *History's* theme; Poe's "freedom from lubricity" and his
unaffected tone depend on that freedom from complex social pressure Wendell calls national inexperience. Poe's "unusual technical
mastery" is never clearly analyzed; but, as Wendell concludes the
chapter, his usual final note of equivocation yields to positive assessment: "Though Poe's power was great, however, his chief merits
prove merits of refinement. Even through a time so recent as his,
refinement of temper, conscientiousness of form, and instinctive
neglect of actual fact remained the most characteristic trait . . . of
American letters" (218).

During Wendell's lectures at the Sorbonne four years later, he
revealed his still growing appreciation of Poe; he even went so far as
to suggest that, if Poe had been motivated by a lyric concern
broader than strangeness and death, "you can hardly avoid wonder-
ing whether Shelley might not have paled beside him." And at the
centennial celebration of Poe's birth at the University of Virginia in
1909, Wendell asserted Poe's "unchallenged" position in permanent
literature.[6] Poe the man may disappear, but Poe the supreme
"dreamer and craftsman" remains,

> The Lunatic, the lover, and the poet
> Are of imagination all compact.

VI *Whitman*

Wendell's long chapter on Whitman demonstrates far more ambivalence and far more struggle than do the chapters on Hawthorne
and Poe; for in it the pressures of his New England predilections,
his aristocratic bias against the working man as the new "privileged"
class, and his conservative interpretation of American democracy
militate against his ability to say anything positive about the Brook-

lyn poet. Indeed, his comments on Whitman evoked heated response from Horace Traubel and sparked a long attack on Wendell
at the international meeting of the Walt Whitman Fellowship in
New York in 1902. The speaker at that gathering saw one more
handicap to Wendell's ability to appreciate Whitman: "We might
once in a while have literature considered from the standpoint of the
man of the world, the man free from academic traditions and un-
dominated by the accepted canons of the literary reviewer."[7] While
the whole *Literary History* shows Wendell struggling to overcome
those very standards, the biases here are clear: Whitman, the son of
a carpenter, grew up in New York "close to the most considerable
and corrupt centre of population on his native continent" (465). His
reading public "was at once limited, fastidiously overcultivated, and
apt to be of foreign birth" (466); and his "dogma of equality" represents clearly a "complete confusion of values" (469).

While in 1893 in *Stelligeri* Wendell's assessment of Whitman is
almost entirely positive, his chapter in 1900 almost threatens to
bury Whitman rather than praise him. He reiterates once more his
belief in the American continuation of English not French political
theory, and he stresses the contradiction of French abstract equality
to natural law, to recorded experience, and certainly to American
practice. Consequently, he can hardly be enthusiastic about Whitman's idea that, "as God made everything, one thing is just as good
as another" (468). Wendell reacts scornfully to the belief of "salvation in the new, life-saving ideal of equality," and he noted ironically
that "among the prophets of equality Whitman has the paradoxical
merit of eminence" (469).

Equally repellent and irritating to Wendell is Whitman's "eccentricity." For instance the famous sixth section of *Song of Myself*
mixes such moving emotions as "beautiful uncut hair of graves" with
"such rubbish" as the "handkerchief of the Lord," the total impression being "an inextricable hodge-podge . . . [of] beautiful phrases
and silly gabble, tender imagination and insolent commonplace"
(471). Wendell finds here a confusion both of poetic and political
values, only compounded by Whitman's eccentricity of form.

Especially on the matter of that form, however, do we see the
ambiguity of Wendell's stance and the possibility in Whitman not of
poetic failure but of innovation. Wendell misreads Whitman's form,
on one hand, when he points out its failure to partake of the "vital
force" of organic development; to Wendell, it fails because the poet

suffers from "inarticulateness" (477). On the other hand, Wendell recalls that successful artistic form often illustrates the high point and final expression of a movement that is past, and then the evolutionary critic of the Shakespeare and seventeenth-century studies reasserts himself here. We remember that Marlowe possessed for Wendell a liberating vision for the still young Elizabethan drama but lacked the mastery of form later so clear in Shakespeare. Whitman Wendell says in *Stelligeri* "lacks form chiefly because he is stammeringly overpowered" by his vision of the future (142). Hart Crane and Ezra Pound, then, might represent the fruition of a line from Whitman which Wendell theoretically could predict.

Though Whitman's vision is powerful, Wendell still wavers: some lines he describes as "confused, inarticulate, and surging in a mad kind of rhythm which sounds as if hexameters were trying to bubble through sewage" (473). And the divergent forces of Wendell's mind almost surface completely in one passage where he shifts from Whitman's "amorphously meaningless" jargon, to his diction that approaches "inevitable union of thought and phrase," to the isolation of such passages, finally to observe that Whitman "leaves you with a sense of new realities concerning which you must do your thinking for yourself "—and all this in one paragraph which indicates that Wendell has entered into the "gymnast's struggle" with the poet, as Whitman described it in the preface to the 1855 edition of *Leaves of Grass*. The Whitman Fellowship speaker felt that Wendell's positive comments on "Crossing Brooklyn Ferry" made his negative assertions seem "hardly to be taken seriously." And indeed in describing the "ideal beauty," the "wonder" of that same poem, Wendell's tone is the most appreciative and his perception the most acute in the whole *History:* "He has found impulses which prove it, like any other region on earth, a fragment of the divine eternities. The glories and beauties of the universe are really perceptible everywhere; and into what seemed utterly sordid Whitman has breathed ennobling imaginative fervor. Cultured and academic folk are disposed to shrink from what they call base, to ignore it, to sneer at it; looking closer, Whitman tells us that even amid base things you cannot wander so far as to lose sight of the heavens" (473).

Whitman's defender had to admit that he knew not whether Whitman's verse form marked "anticipation of what the future will prefer and adopt";[8] but, to Wendell, Whitman "seems not only native but even promising" (478). Interestingly, Wendell does not conclude the chapter directly in his own words; he chooses to quote, without citation, a favorable comment from his earlier *Stelligeri:*

"He is uncouth, inarticulate, whatever you please that is least orthodox; yet, after all, he can make you feel for the moment how even ferry-boats plying from New York to Brooklyn are fragments of God's eternities. Those of us who love the past are far from sharing his confidence in the future. Surely, however, that is no reason for denying the miracle that he has wrought by idealising the East River. The man who has done this is the only one who points out the stuff of which perhaps the new American literature of the future may in time be made." (479)

In Wendell's later lectures, this positive note grew stronger. At the Sorbonne, while pointing to Whitman's adherence to the wrong brand of democracy—the mediocrity of equality—he pointed out that Whitman's vivid descriptive power and his sensitivity to surrounding life force us "to admit that he possessed a spark of what we call genius." And to his classes he delivered whole lectures on Whitman with only a single sentence of negativity, and he characterized Whitman as the forerunner of "a spirit that may inspire that [future] literature with meaning not to be sought in other worlds than this western world of ours."[9]

We have dwelt longest on Whitman in this chapter because his life, career, and beliefs placed him at opposite poles from Barrett Wendell, a critic who resorts even to the odd circumlocution of anonymously quoting himself in a positive voice, a supposed anglophile merely paying lip service to American literature in his book, who makes his most positive assessments against the overwhelming back pressure of his personal prejudices.

VII *Later Reevaluations*

The same kind of critical integrity that forced Wendell's critical assessment of Whitman leads Wendell back years after the *Literary History* to revise his earlier estimates of Poe and Whitman, and also to comment in his 1904 school edition of the *Literary History* on the still-living authors omitted in 1900.[10] Even his later lectures reveal the increased respect for men who earlier suffered from the narrowness of Wendell's Brahmin bias. Nonetheless he hardly does more than list many of the major names with a brief sentence or two of comment: Emily Dickinson—the only time her name appears in his work—"laments a vanished past almost as palpably as the mood of Transcendentalism welcomed an unfathomable future," though in "hauntingly mournful tones" (391).

In the contemporary novel, Wendell discovers vitality in several writers, and he makes clear at the same time some of his critical standards: realist Howells writes "patient, insistent, yet often brilliant studies of average men and women." That his novels, in Wendell's view, are marred by a lifelong "diffidence" shows the Harvard historian's distaste for the euphemistic aspects of contemporary literature, for a timidity which involves even the external, realistic style of Howells's work and forbids "a feeling of intimate familiarity even with the scene and people of his own creation" (396–97). He similarly faults Henry James's "insidious overrefinement of both thought and style," but he praises James's international novel which sets "the character of America face to face with the older civilization of Europe," as the "most noteworthy" of contemporary fiction; he believes "none is more masterly" than James (397–98).

Wendell also admires the work of Edith Wharton, whose concern and form seem distinctly superior in "vivid power of imagination, more firm grasp of subject, more punctilious master of style, or more admirably pervasive artistic conscience" (367). And Frank Norris has "startling power" in work modeled on Zola that before the American writer's death made him seem "destined to be the most powerful novelist in our country." In the South, he singles out Joel Chandler Harris's "remarkable sketches," and in the West the "vitality and vivacity" and the "skillfully artistic form" of Bret Harte.

The man who ties all these regions together, however, is the local-color realist Mark Twain, "the real, and perhaps a great, exponent of the actual temper of our people." In the school edition, an entire chapter is devoted to Mark Twain so that Wendell can show not only how he "completely exemplifies the kind of humor which is most characteristically American—a shrewd sense of fact expressing itself in an inextricable confusion of literal statement and wild extravagance" (422)—but can also say that *Huckleberry Finn* is "nothing short of a masterpiece" and that it is "among the few books in any literature which preserve something like a comprehensive picture of an entire state of society" (422). In the *Literary History*, of course, Mark Twain, as still living, was off limits; but his presence even there intrudes several times illustrating Wendell's admiration.

Commenting, for instance, on Whitman's language experiment, he remembers the occasional attempts in literature to capture the American idiom: "This impulse has resulted in at least one masterpiece, that amazing Odyssey of the Mississippi to which Mark Twain gave the fantastic name 'Huckleberry Finn' " (477). The work of Mark Twain, which would have been exceptional anywhere, results for Wendell in literature that is "characteristically American" (513).

VIII   *"The Dusk of Dawn"*

Wendell laments the passing of old New England, its homogeneous values, its certainty, and its "purity" of thought and feeling. But he cannot pronounce the *dies irae* on that tradition as the end of real American literature since Mark Twain, a figure essentially western, points to a new day. The tragedy of American innocence, of American inexperience, lies in the inevitable growing up that must come—the initiation into experience. We have seen in the twentieth century a spate of literature based not just on the older theme of Ishmael's encounter with Ahab, Huck's with a harsh society, or Isabel Archer's with Europe, but the confrontation of the American dream itself with the "foul dust" that trails in its wake. For Wendell, the end of the nineteenth century marked the growing pressures of materialism and the heterogeneous values of new immigrants which threatened to bury forever the old inexperience. With regard to New England's renaissance, Wendell, the evolutionary critic who believed that the lasting literary expressions "are the final expression of things almost past" (as in Periclean Greece, Augustan Rome, Shakespearian England [462]), could see beyond the passing of New England to New York, the South, the West, as regions only beginning to give voice to a newer culture: "Only the passing of old New England made its literature possible. The great material prosperity of New York, meanwhile, has attracted thither during the past forty years countless numbers of energetic people from all over the world. . . . Our new metropolis, in fact, is not only far from such a stage of decline as should mark the beginning of its passage from life to history, but it has not even formed the tangible traditions which may by and by define its spiritual character (462–63).

Even of New England he wonders whether 1900 revealed a decline or a stage preparing for a literature of the future. He sees that future partially in Walt Whitman, the poet who indicated the

material of that new literature, who grew up not in inexperienced
New England but in the growing city of New York in a new environment of experience not yet ready for literary expression: "Whitman's earthy experience, then, came throughout in chaotic times,
when our past had faded and our future had not yet sprung into
being. Bewildering confusion, fused by the accident of his lifetime
into the seeming unity of a momentary whole, was the only aspect of
human existence which could be afforded him by the native country
which he so truly loved. . . . His lifelong eagerness to find in life
the stuff of which poetry is made has brought him, after all, the
reward he would most have cared for. In one aspect he is
thoroughly American" (478). The confusing elements of modern industrial America, of a developing world power—growth, change,
energy—these, Wendell feared, predicted the course of the future;
but that modern world, like inexperienced New England, would
soon produce its poets and a literature of maturity.

As for the South, Wendell's survey uncovers little he can accord
first-rate significance; yet "as one thinks . . . of Dr. Ticknor, of
Hayne, of Timrod, and of Lanier, one begins to wonder whether
they may not perhaps forerun a spirit which shall give beauty and
power to the American letters of the future" (499). Based on his own
observation of the West and its still-young literature, Wendell
sees that "this great confused West has not yet developed such
unity of character as has marked our elder regions" but is "a region from which in time to come we may hope for a broader and
more superbly imaginative expression than any which America
has hitherto known" (506); and Mark Twain represents something of
that literary hope.

What Wendell anticipates here is not simply the fruition of local-
color traditions. At times we suspect his fear for America's literary
future evolves from the loss of the particular New England values of
idealism, the New England which is "the microcosm of the America
to come." But Wendell, at the conclusion of the *Literary History*,
does not anticipate any special sectional literature but sees the
growth of a national literature: "The America of the future, however, seems likely to be a country in which the forces which have
gathered separately may finally fuse into a centralised nationality
more conscious and more powerful than we have yet known" (514).
The negativity so often noted in the *Literary History* is muted by the
voice that foresees a future in American literature still possessing
"the youthful features of vitality and of hopefulness."

Paul Elmer More said of the *History* that Wendell seemed to have avoided the error of making too much about a literature as yet of "trivial magnitude" and in "avoiding it has perhaps gone to the other extreme." Still, More felt that Wendell "has kept the connection between literature and history very skillfully in view. I think his emphasis on our 'national inexperience' and on the fact that we have . . . lagged behind England and Europe, as a reason for a lack of literature, is quite just." Wendell's Boston quality he found refreshing if obviously snobbish, and his "historical sense . . . this sense of the connection of literature and society seems to me to give the book a certain mark of maturity."[11] More concluded his comment, however, by characteristically complaining that Wendell lacked spiritual insight into history and therefore missed much of the importance of men like Emerson.

More's words are interesting because they reveal the same ambivalences toward Wendell's *Literary History* that we find in Howells's inability to accept Wendell's tone toward those New England writers that Howells still admired and his proclamation, nonetheless, of the book's importance. Wendell appreciated the idealistic energy of the old Puritans but felt himself cut off from any religious value. He respected the thrust of American literature but saw things in terms of the wider perspective of European historical and critical values. He distrusted the amateurism implicit in the older impressionist criticism but could never embrace the pedantry of new Germanic scholarship. What logically resulted is a book of strengths and weaknesses, relative to particular conceptions about the nature of literary history.

The weak points of Wendell's study are clear. In the first place, we could say that Wendell just did not know enough about his subject, since we keep wishing for evidence at times to support rather glib generalizations (though Fred Lewis Pattee still wondered in 1928 "what the story of American literature will look like when all the documents fully are in").[12] Perry Miller, describing Moses Coit Tyler's strength as a historian, put his finger on one of Wendell's biggest weaknesses, however: growing up in Michigan, Tyler came East as a scholar and maintained "his membership in both the older and the newer civilizations"; as "the colonist, the exile from the maternal culture [he] revisited the old in order to appreciate his position as a citizen of the new."[13] Wendell, on the other hand, came of age in isolated Boston when he entered by accident what he felt to be the sterile atmosphere of Cambridge.

Consequently, while he never felt great enthusiasm for Boston, his provincial heritage, as well as his physical and emotional weakness, cut him off from sympathy with the rough, crude frontier America booming beyond the Mississippi River. While Tyler's judgment came from a certainty of taste and a deep sympathy with his material, Wendell was a man of mixed sympathy and of mixed eclectic tastes. W. P. Eaton assessed his former teacher thus: "America needed to be discovered anew, by minds of a different cast. . . . He was born too much of a Tory, too much under the shadow of the Lowell family tree. . . . His, perhaps, is the common tragedy of the Tory artist, in an expanding and changing world."[14]

Yet we have seen strengths, too. Howard Mumford Jones concludes in *The Theory of American Literature* that *"the constant and characteristic element in American literary history has been the search for a formula rather than the solution of a metaphysical problem."*[15] While Wendell may not emphasize the highly elaborate quality of American culture, his thesis of national inexperience attempts to answer questions like Norman Foerster's later, "In what sense is our literature distinctively American?" "What are the local conditions of life and thought in America that produce these results?"[16] And, as far as Wendell's method goes, Harry Hayden Clark's survey of the early literary histories led him to state that they impress "the reader with the fact that most of modern theories of approach were stated in one way or another long ago." He found that Wendell's comparative method and his sense of American culture produced "one of the best of the earlier comprehensive books," and that, before the knowledge of the new economists and historians, Wendell made "a brave attempt at our modern methods of analyses."[17]

Wendell was a man whose touchstones, like those of his teacher Lowell, were the classics: Homer, Dante, Shakespeare; and he was a man who tried honestly to write a history of American literature with a valid thesis. We may turn once more to Wendell's view of his teacher Lowell for a clue to his own difficulty in this task: "The most truly human," Wendell writes in the *Literary History*, is he who attempts to comprehend "the records of the past to which we give the name of the humanities," but the "most deeply human" is he who attempts to "understand the humanity around him": "It was unceasing effort to fuse his understanding of the humanities with his understanding of humanity which made Lowell so often seem paradoxical. He was in constant doubt as to which of these influences signified the more; and this doubt so hampered his power of expression that the merit of his writing lies mostly in disjointed phrases" (406).

Perhaps as we have examined the structure of Wendell's *Literary History*, his thesis seems disjointed; but insofar as he attempts to organize the work around this thesis of national inexperience his study is a real history. National inexperience, despite the pressure of serious prejudice, is central. It is overworked, and it is defensive; it is even outrageous at times in its oversimplification. Nonetheless, Wendell's view of inexperience and the more recent thesis of American innocence largely parallel each other; the latter, like any historical principle of order, is just as reductive as the former, and Wendell's is not less viable. National inexperience does not mean, any more than does American innocence, that there was no American experience, no American guilt; it does mean that America forever maintained its provinciality, its innocence, its ideality. The audacity of writing in 1900 America—progressive, wild-eyed with mission and social betterment, and full of high-toned Christian old women—a literary history arguing inexperience from a sense of despair at its passing has a real parallel two decades later when Theodore Dreiser demonstrated the dissolution of the American Dream into the American Tragedy and when the American expatriate F. Scott Fitzgerald created a tale about a man named Gatsby who believed he could recapture a lost innocence and about Gatsby's historian Nick Carroway who sees a future that ever recedes into the past.

CHAPTER 7

Light-Giver: The Harvard Professor

THE cloak of irony and self-depreciation that Wendell wore and the cloak of gentility thrown over him by later writers are full of holes. Beneath this ragged costume of Tory, Brahmin, antiquarian, and eccentric stands a more engaging personality—the innovator in education, the inspiring teacher, the disseminator of tradition, and a link with a usable past. If Adams and Wendell saw in the new century a world they could not like or accept, the rebellion that reached a crescendo by the 1920s was engineered and directed by men like Van Wyck Brooks and T. S. Eliot, who, while at Harvard, had been fed a diet of rebellion by teachers too weak to rebel themselves. Harvard, like Chicago, became a major source of creative energy in the new literary activity, even though much of that energy arose in reaction: Robert Frost quit Harvard after two years, Edwin Arlington Robinson never finished, and Brooks dismissed the whole Cambridge milieu. But, as William James maintained, "our undisciplinables are our proudest products."

I *One of the Great Teachers*

Hardly just a scene of genteel sterility and abstraction, turn-of-the-century Cambridge contained no less than five different Harvards: a national center of vigorous reform in education, an international center of research, the "parochial pleasure-ground of the clubmen," an influential teaching institution, and the "mecca of the disaffected young men who wanted to write."[1] While the "second" Harvard comprised the work of Francis Child, George Lyman Kittredge, and Fred Robinson, and while the third group (the Roosevelts, the "Hollis Alworthy's") enjoyed Barrett Wendell's after-dinner wit, educational reform, sound teaching, and creative youth absorbed Wendell's serious attention at Harvard for thirty-seven years. Indeed, he was either famous or infamous for those four decades to nearly every kind of Harvard undergraduate and graduate student. In the 1926 volume of essays dedicated to Wendell's memory, William Castle best described this well-known teacher: "Some scoffed at Wendell, some were afraid of him, a few laughed at him; but his enduring monument is the army of men who were inspired by him to high thinking; who were helped by him to understand the fullness and the richness of life; who, in their turn, have become light-givers."[2]

Wendell's appointment at Harvard came through an accidental meeting with A. S. Hill in 1880; and, as we have noted, he was never comfortable with the more professionally oriented graduate students, the Germanic methods of scholarship, or President Charles Eliot's innovative and influential elective curriculum. Moreover, Wendell fought continually a bewildered distaste for his academic work, and he increasingly despaired over its quality. Nevertheless, as H. L. Mencken stated, Wendell "opened paths that he was unable to traverse himself. Sturdier men, following him, were soon marching far ahead of him."[3] The perspective of Wendell at Harvard which needs emphasis, then, is that revealed by Samuel Eliot Morison when describing the "great teachers" at Harvard: "One naturally thinks of Wendell, who . . . endeavored to develop individuality and freshness . . . , who under a more or less transparent mask of contrariness and eccentricity united creative power with sound critical sense."[4]

It may have been that "power," the flux in higher education, or the rapid growth of new courses that caused Wendell to teach some twenty different courses at Harvard from 1884 to 1917. With only the Bachelor of Arts degree and with no specialized training, Wendell represents the older college teacher in his versatility: he taught everything from Beowulf to the present—survey courses, courses in Shakespeare, Renaissance drama, Elizabethan literature, Jacobean drama, Spenser, the seventeenth and eighteenth centuries, the romantics, comparative literature courses from Homer to Kipling, composition courses, and the first course in American literature at Harvard. Two of his more popular courses were perhaps the first of their kind to be offered in American universities: in 1887, he first taught English 14, The Drama Exclusive of Shakespeare, from the Miracle Plays to the Closing of the Theaters. And his very popular English 23, Shakespeare, he offered first at Radcliffe in 1884 and took to Harvard in 1892, teaching it with regularity until his retirement.

But one of Wendell's major contributions lies in the area of rhetoric and composition. In general, we remember the Harvard of the turn of the century because of the large presence of Kittredge, and for obvious reasons; the climate of philological interest and scholarly orientation which Kittredge effectively promoted by the example of imaginative textual criticism remains the climate in professional academic circles today. Composition courses connote drudge work from which it is desirable to be excused, as only Child and Kittredge were excused in those last years of the old century. Yet the teaching of freshman composition remains an essential task of the English Department, and the roots of that course as taught today are to be found, in both inception and method, in that same philologically famous Harvard. Samuel Eliot Morison says that the two most important dates in the development of the English Department are 1884 when Wendell began his famous and "distinguished" English 12 course in elective composition and 1885 when Wendell began teaching Adams Sherman Hill's English 5 course in advanced composition.[5]

II *English Composition*

Writing in 1908 about the situation in composition when his career began, Wendell said, "Little attention was given to this fine art at American colleges, and American students wrote badly," but in the subsequent thirty years, all that had changed; now "the catalogue of almost any American college will show you an offering of instruction in composition."[6] And Harvard led the way. In 1884, composition became a university requirement; and Wendell's sophomore English 12 became a magnet for students who wished to develop their talent as writers. Wendell's famous book *English Composition* (1891) derived from his composition courses and his Lowell Institute lectures on the subject. It presents in essay form the way words, sentences, and paragraphs go into the making of whole compositions according to the principles of unity, or central idea; mass, or external form; and coherence, or internal arrangement and the demands of style: intellectual clearness, emotional force, and aesthetic elegance.[7]

Wendell's concerns with English composition may be seen from two angles—his technique in teaching the course and the theory which underlies that technique. In the first place, he was little concerned with rhetoric and with the memorization of rules. Herein he departed from his teacher Hill whose practice in his *Principles of Rhetoric* (1876) was to move from examples to specific rules inductively.[8] Wendell preferred, on the other hand, to begin deductively with the effect desired and to employ whatever rhetorical technique was necessary to achieve that result. In his teaching, rules gave way to general principles, and consequently his technique amounted to an emphasis on actual writing. Therefore, the technique that was to become famous and synonymous with his name was the daily theme. The student was directed to keep a daily record of things most meaningful to him in his own experience, for Wendell's concern was not only with writing but with the source of all written expression, life itself.

His emphasis on the whole theme is apparent in comparison with Hill's *Rhetoric*, in which the organization carries the student from words to sentences to paragraphs. Although Wendell takes that same route, the distinction for him is the whole composition. And this extra step in Wendell's procedure underlines a basic difference in the two approaches, illustrates why Wendell called himself "rather heretical," and points to a serious misreading of his basic position by later critics. A central problem for both Hill and Wendell is "Good Usage." Hill says, "It is the business of grammars to record and to classify expressions that are approved by good use" (30), whereas Wendell writes, "To the state of things which enables us to decide . . . what the case is at any given moment, we give, for convenience sake, the name 'Good Use' " (13). When we investigate the difference between these two statements, we see that Hill maintains that "the decisions of good use are final" (30) and that Wendell repeatedly stresses fluidity—"The limits of good use are wide and flexible" (17). Good use, "like all other vital things, not only comes into being and flourishes, but it passes out of being too" (18). The essence of good use is "that it is not a system of rules, but a constantly shifting state of fact" (26), for it is important to remember that "the agreement of good use is not precise, but approximate" (viii).

The mistake is, therefore, to identify Wendell's "good use" with "correct use" and thus to dismiss him as a scourge of improprieties. We can indeed fault Wendell's use of reputable, national, and present as final standards—like Hill—to determine good use; and certainly Wendell the genteel critic speaks in the single passage in which he condemns Maupassant for describing "according to our standards . . . very abominable subjects" (293), subjects about which "the better plan is to ask ourselves whether we may not best of all leave . . . unmentioned" (296). When we cite Wendell for squeamishness, we do so at the expense of the Wendell who is caught somewhere between this Victorian attitude and the stance which decried euphemisms as aesthetically degrading in literature (296)—the Wendell within whom warred a didactic humanism and an aesthetic creativity. The critic must ascertain a writer's purpose before attacking his methods, and "the purpose of not a few admirable artists is so detestable that on grounds of morality and decency we may utterly condemn their work; but this fact does not, in my opinion, at all affect the value of their work as a work of art" (292–93). In this statement we find the Howellsian conflict between larger aesthetic standards and more provincial didactic ones, but, when Wendell feels this conflict in expression, his final concern with whole compositions throws the emphasis on the aesthetic side, for "good use" works as a principle rather inflexibly on the level of words, "relaxes" its authority on the level of sentence structure, becomes very "feeble" in the construction of paragraphs, and gives way altogether in the whole composition to the matter, not of right or wrong, but of good or better—to the question of "how accurately it expresses what the writer has to say" (38–39, 2).

Wendell is hardly just the genteel nay-sayer. Even in *English Composition* on the strictest level of good usage he passes over barbaric and improper words as those either made up, obsolete, or inexact (44–50); otherwise, word choice—Latin or Saxon, long or short, literal or figurative—is simply a matter of desired effect (50–62). And on the sentence level, with regard to the ever-present problem of choice between *it is me* and *it is I*, Wendell, one of the first to make this descriptive distinction about syntax, writes: "Everyone knows that the latter form is logically the true one; most of us have been reproved over and over again for our depraved persistency in the use of the former. But, as a matter of fact, has not good use gone a long way to make *it is me* idiomatic, and *it is I* a bit pedantic? I do not feel at all sure that we can answer *No*" (80). Wendell's overriding concern in composition is as modern now as when he stated it: "What is the effect I wish to produce, and how may I best produce it?" (147). Effective style continually emerges out of the conflict between the choice of techniques and the desired effect.

To bring the intellectual powers into balance with the forces of the world around us was for Wendell the purpose of education, and his object in English 12 included not only good expression but an awakening of the students' awareness: "What I bid them chiefly try for is that each [daily] record shall tell something that makes the day on which it is made different from the day before," with the result that "each new bundle of these daily notes that I take up proves a fresh whiff of real human life . . . ; and as the months go on, more and more of these boys begin to find out for themselves how far from monotonous a thing even the routine of a college life may be if you will only use your eyes to see and your ears to hear."

Important here is Wendell's definition of style as the written expression of thought and feeling, the ideas and emotions representing the "final reality of life," the "immaterial reality" which could be construed as a "distrust of materialism" and as a retreat into ideality if we did not read Wendell writing to Robert Herrick in 1889 about the realistic novelists: "They photograph when they should paint," he says, but he qualifies that statement by adding, "but they are on the right track."[9] And he urged that same track on his composition students when he told them to look through their own eyes, to express their own "thought and feelings," and to draw their material from "actual experience." The dual emphasis of attending to immediate experience and relying on personal response to such experience fuses in writing as ". . . one of those feats that tell us why men have believed that God made man in His image. For he who scrawls ribaldry, just as truly as he who writes for all time, does that most wonderful of all things,—gives a material body to some reality which till that moment was immaterial, executes, all unconscious of the power for which divine is none too grand a word, a lasting act of creative imagination" (40).

Such was the theory behind one of the most popular electives at Harvard. Its instructor was as eccentric in speech as in appearance; he was the author of two novels; his was the text; and he cared seriously about the individual student—as such, Barrett Wendell's prestige was enormous with undergraduates. His office in Grays 18 housed both the feared taskmaster and respected counselor. The picture characteristic of Wendell for his former students is that in Mark A. DeWolfe Howe's biography: the young professor sits in that famous office, his desk overflowing with the themes which he corrected "with zest and sympathy, pinning down the faults with a biting phrase, or drawing out any flair for true observation or delightful style with keen and judicious commendation."[10] Students remembered that Wendell minimized the unattractiveness of those compositions, and George Baker summarized the feelings of many students when he said that it was "really as a teacher of English composition that he did his greatest work. Those who know well his book on English composition may find in it the clear portrait of a great teacher. . . . With him we did not think of writing as a matter of rules; he helped us find something we wanted to say: then he helped us say it well, but above all, in our own ways."[11]

The influence of Wendell's innovations in composition was great. In the late nineteenth century, Harvard and President Eliot spoke to the national education establishment with the voice of authority. What happened at Harvard was watched attentively; and Wendell's book, his students, and then their books carried his approach to every part of the nation. Newspapers and magazines wrote excitedly about the educational value of the "daily theme eye," and teacher demand for more information about Harvard's theme courses led to the addition of a "Note for Teachers" in reprintings of *English Composition;* to another book, *The Forms of English Prose* (1900), begun by Wendell and completed by his assistant John Gardiner; and to Charles Copeland and H. M. Rideout's *Freshman English and Theme Correcting in Harvard College* (1901).

The number of books based on Wendell's theory and methods is uncountable, and the attitudes toward composition that underlie texts and courses today express tacit indebtedness to that same influence. Lucia Mirrielees in 1937 said to teachers that Wendell's book "is sound in principle but not formally given. A host of textbooks have been founded on it, but as an adult you might well seek the original."[12] Even Wendell himself could write in *The Privileged Classes* (1909), "this not very important book has proved a landmark. . . . It has stood the test of time" (163–64). Though it was imitated all over the country and cited as a model text, the *English Composition* itself was in print as a text until 1942. George Santayana said succinctly: "A change of tone [in American writing] there has certainly been in the last thirty years; and who knows how much of it may not be due to Barrett Wendell?"[13]

III   *American Literature*

We have treated at some length this aspect of Wendell's teaching career, but it is by no means the most striking feature of that career. Robert Herrick has marked the pathway of our attention from Wendell's influence in composition to this work in literature:

The immense effort put forth in American schools and colleges to teach the art of writing is more directly attributable to Barrett Wendell than to any other. . . . The ideal stands . . . of unremitting industry, of practice and pains. And a vivid realisation that the least of expression may yet be creation.

The reverse effort of interpreting the creation of literature in terms of humanity, as it was begotten, owes hardly less to the example and practice of Barrett Wendell.[14]

The man whose twentieth-century reputation casts him as the arch-villain of American literary studies created not only courses that promoted creative activity but one of the first university courses in American literature. Such courses and American literature texts appeared throughout the nineteenth century, like John Neel's *American Writers* in 1824, and John S. Hart's course at the College of New Jersey in 1872. Some thirty-nine schools taught American literature prior to 1900, and those mostly in the 1890s when there occurred "an awakening on the part of many colleges and universities to the possibilities of American literature"[15]—possibilities in most cases to teach literature on an *ad hoc* basis with American history, politics, law, or with English Victorian literature.

Wendell's name has missed the attention it deserves among the ranks of that small handful generally associated with the rising interest in American literature (Joseph W. Beach at Minnesota, William P. Trent at Columbia, William Cairns at Wisconsin, Fred Lewis Pattee at Pennsylvania State, Moses Coit Tyler at Michigan and Cornell, Arthur H. Quinn at Pennsylvania). The "indifferent success" of late nineteenth-century American literature courses was not shared at Harvard, where in 1897, when Wendell was department chairman, he began his reading course English 20c, Research in the Literary History of America; he offered it continuously (except for Wendell's years in England and France) to undergraduates (and from 1911 to graduates) until his retirement in 1917.

As usual, the results of a course became the basis for a book—this time the famous *Literary History of America*, which, with its school edition, *A History of Literature in America* (1904), remained in print into the 1940s. Its influence was widespread, and, to a great extent, negative. Wendell nevertheless was one of the first serious instructors of American literature and his *Literary History*, "partly on account of its very faults of proportion and of judgment, aroused very useful counter-blasts and greatly advanced the prestige of its subject in American colleges."[16]

Closely related to Wendell's interest in American literature and his belief in the dynamic interrelationship of literature and life was Wendell's concern with interdisciplinary studies and with the systematic concentration of undergraduate instruction. This concern arose, in part, as reaction against President Eliot's elective system, and we meet again the typically paradoxical Wendell who urged individual thought and expression but who in curriculum was leary of a system that allowed individuality to govern a student's program of study. The success of President Eliot's plan was such that Wendell's generation at Harvard turned to General Education as a remedy. Wendell shared the feeling that by 1900 "something disastrous had happened at Harvard College, however proud one felt about what President Eliot had done to make it Harvard University." What resulted, then, was an effort to balance the old classical tradition of general learning with the new specialization method, an attempt to reestablish the concept of developing the whole man. And, while the General Education movement is sometimes dated at Columbia University in 1919, its seeds were germinating at Harvard around the turn of the century. Wendell, who felt the elective system wasteful and bewildering, found his views about this "careless scattering of undergraduate effort" shared by Abbott Lawrence Lowell in government, Charles Haskins and Roger Merriman in history, William Schofield in comparative literature, and Chester Greenough in English; and, as a result, the honors program in literature and history, formulated as an attempt to give definite structure to past achievement, became "a pioneering reality at Cambridge . . . and actually foreshadowed the shape and substance of the pattern of much of the General Education persuasion in approach."[17]

Though Wendell's *Literary History* preceded the anthropological, psychological, and economic interpretations of modern history, his work in the interdisciplinary program at Harvard reveals the same reasoning and creativity of that earlier work. And, just as the fact of Wendell's *History* as an essay in national culture has been lost in regrets about its Brahmin prejudices, so the real thrust of the Harvard history-literature degree is overlooked by historians of American Studies programs. J. D. Spaeth's Literary History of American Ideals course may have been epoch making in 1919 at Columbia, and serious study of the American civilization may not have begun until the 1930s; but the cooperation of political science, history, and literature under the leadership at Harvard of Barrett Wendell emerges as the major precursor of twentieth-century programs in American Studies. While Wendell's legacy is larger than this one program, Alan Heimert notes the importance of the program when he writes that at his death Wendell's "surviving monument was Harvard's undergraduate honors field of History and Literature."[18]

IV   *A Teacher's Influence*

Wendell forever emphasized in class "that literature, like mankind, is—however produced—a living, feeling thing." That his students left his classes with this view is the overwhelming evidence of their letters, their books, their autobiographies. Robert Herrick's comment is typical when he described Wendell as having the "rich flavor, personal and eccentric, that youth delights in."[19] At worst, Wendell impressed students as an overly eccentric, opinionated personality; neutrally, he appeared as a distinguished professor who seemed to bring into the classroom the aroma of the great world outside. It appears that for many students "Wendy" was not classified among the usual impersonal procession of instructors, that initial reaction to Wendell's mannerisms gave way to the awareness of personal warmth, and that in his room in Grays 18 he provided personal advice as well as sound criticism. To his classes, Wendell presented an amalgam of impulsiveness, nervousness, sensitivity, wit, irony, and heresy.

Certainly there were students whom Wendell repelled; but such students, according to the more positive reminiscence of their classmates, were the conventional and intolerant. There was something playful about Wendell's mind; he was always posturing to shatter illusions and undisputed authority, to reveal hypocrisy, and to stimulate individual thinking. He embodied the irony of a man whom critics and indeed his own self-portrait depict as hating change and who at the same time committed himself to the most liberal of goals, the encouragement of students to think for themselves. In his composition courses, as he writes in *English Composition*, he cared less whether students learned how to write than that they acquired "this real knowledge of individual awareness and response" (266). For all his aristocratic tendencies and his love for the "gentle past," he was a rebel: "He was witheringly intolerant of the conventional for its own sake, moral-timidity, the commonplace, or worship of the letter instead of the spirit."[20]

It is easy to see in retrospect that, while Van Wyck Brooks and Bernard DeVoto (both former students) condemned the Barrett Wendells for not giving them a program for revolution, the older Harvard nonetheless gave them the weapons with which to rebel. Wendell was sentimental about the past, but he knew it "the most delusive of irridescent fantasies" to hope for its return. He hated the ugliness of reform-conscious America; but, seeing the job of education as an effort to achieve "the nearest possible adjustment of man to his environment," he urged his students to question the past and to attend to the present.

Behind all of these concerns seems to lie "Wendell's outstanding distinction as a teacher—that he made his students feel the inevitable relationship between the things he taught and the lives they lived."[21] This awareness of interdependency Wendell attributes to his former professor Charles Eliot Norton: "I find myself year by year trying to conduct [my work] more and more in the spirit you taught me years ago;—trying to keep before the students the relation to actual life and conduct the work they are doing. . . . I know more and more the value of the sympathetic council you gave me as a student."[22] We have seen the academic innovations in composition and comparative studies produced by this attitude, and its "process to humanize" is directly apparent in the testimony of former students Walter Eaton and George Baker.

For Eaton, Wendell's epigrammatic wit "has come back to me, with its twinge of wordly wisdom and its cynical realism, far more often than any of the learned lucubrations of Professor Kittredge."[23] How striking it is also to compare the version of Wendell as a genteel conservative clinging to an outworn Boston literature and ignoring a dynamic present with Baker's words: "Those were the days when colleges studied only the works of men safely dead, and most of us were far too ready to take our literary opinions as matters of long standing. To listen to his mind playing about some well-known book was to gain new insight into it, to be roused to fierce combating for his antagonizing views, and to be made to think for ourselves."[24]

When we consider the students who studied under Wendell, we may agree with Wendell when he claims in *The Privileged Classes*, "there is vastly less dissipation of human energy now because of what may sometimes seem the tragic failures of the past" (267)—the kind of "failure" typified by Henry Adams, E. C. Stedman, Wendell, and others who were unable to break the bonds of an outworn tradition, but whose efforts helped another generation to do so. The list of men who followed Wendell is both impressive and ironic since the success of their work meant the eclipsing of their former teachers: George Santayana, Joel Spingarn, Van Wyck Brooks, John Macy, T. S. Eliot, John Dos Passos, V. L. Parrington are men whose work marks the emergence of a new criticism and creativity in the twentieth century, and they are major representatives of generations of men who studied ". . . under the guidance of a fastidious instructor who was always watchful for individuality, for fine phrasing, for craftsmanship . . . , a source of profound stimulation. It was not 'scholarly' inspiration. It was not as an educational process that they felt the work. It was an artistic, or creative, inspiration."[25]

V *Toward Scholarship*

Wendell's inspiration was both scholarly and artistic. His encouragement to his student John Lomax's work with cowboy ballads, his discussion of the ballads with Lomax reading them in the American literature class, his praise of the work for shedding light on the "laws of literature" which in turn would aid the study of other ballads lie behind the long career of Lomax and his son in the cowboy ballad tradition.[26] John M. Manly, Wendell's first graduate student, who at the University of Chicago was to build a superb English Department, also expressed indebtedness to Wendell for giving him "three of the most valuable things a teacher can give a student: ideas, inspiration to independent thinking, and an example of the possibility and value of seeing a work of literature under both its historical and its permanent aspects."[27] Wendell the Shakespeare professor introduced Manly to the knowledge of English drama that became the basis for his own course later at Chicago. In the introduction to his *Specimens of the Pre-Shaksperian Drama*, Manly noted that "Professor Barrett Wendell, of Harvard University, nearly ten years ago first awakened my interest in the subject of these volumes. In the Introduction he will doubtless recognize, as his own, ideas which, after the lapse of so long a time, I am unable to credit to their rightful owner."[28]

Karl Young, whose *Drama of the Medieval Church* is still a standard, also spoke highly of his former teacher: "Your ardor and masterly art . . . are with me permanently as a guide in writing and as a reminder in teaching." For Columbia Professor Algernon Tassin, who tried to pattern his teaching on Wendell's, his old professor "did me more good than all the rest of them [at Harvard] put together." Ashley Thorndike, the author of his own rhetoric text and the editor of the Tudor Shakespeare, spoke of his "loyalty to literature" gained from Wendell.[29] And the well-known Yale Professor William Lyon Phelps, also a former student, assistant, and lifetime friend of Wendell whose interest in American literature he took to Yale, expressed his indebtedness and fondness for Wendell in his *Autobiography* (1939). Another scholar who followed Wendell's work in American literature was Kenneth B. Murdock, Harvard's first director of doctoral studies in that field, who praised Wendell's *Cotton Mather* as "so excellent a study of its difficult subject as to make quite superfluous any attempt to rewrite the tale."[30] Even scholars who were students of Wendell's through his books praised him: Sir Arthur T. Quiller-Couch called Wendell his "star among Shakespearian scholars" and dedicated his *Shakespeare's Workmanship* to Wendell "in gratitude for many pleasures of insight directed by his illuminating common sense."[31]

Scholars in other fields, too, expressed indebtedness and appreciation for Wendell. E. K. Rand, long a classical scholar and first editor of *Speculum*, called Wendell his "master," a "keen-eyed critic of the page."[32] But Horace M. Kallen—immigrant Jewish philosopher, the founder of the New School for Social Research, and a colleague of Thorstein Veblen, Charles Beard, and James Harvey Robinson—has offered the most striking testimony to Wendell's concerns and effects as a teacher. His lifelong friendship, according to Kallen, "stood the test of radical divergences in outlook and aspiration to the very end," and those differences were major between the conservative Bostonian and the Jew with positive concerns for labor and for the problems of minorities who advocated American pluralism and who supported the American Civil Liberties Union. The liberal Kallen, perhaps more than any other of his students, illustrates the ideal results of Wendell's principles: "He freed my surprised mind for ways of perceiving the American Idea and for the art of saying anything I saw which gave a new turn to my appraisal of myself as a free man among other men. I learned soon that the figure of this man of letters, with his cane and his pince-nez, his difficult articulation . . . and the tory-like stance of his protesting spirit, shaped up, in the sight of many, as exaggerated snobbery. I found this a superficial if not an illusory image."[33]

Howe's book reveals the length of their warm correspondence, but Kallen's books show a debt to Wendell's ideas; and his progressive *Culture and Democracy in the United States* (1924) expresses the influence explicitly: "To the memory of Barrett Wendell, Poet, Teacher, Man of Letters, Deep Seeing Interpreter of America and the American Mind, in whose teaching I perceived my first vision of their trends and meanings, I reverently dedicate this book." Under men like Wendell, Kallen found "an unexpected confirmation of the heart's vision which the brain could understand," and "developed the literary and analytical qualities that later were to distinguish his career as an independent thinker."[34]

One of the more important figures in American literature influenced thus was George Pierce Baker, and again the concern with the close relationship between literature and life appears central to the influence. Wendell's interest in drama extended beyond his courses in medieval and Elizabethan plays, and his own plays were written as "frank experiments in the Elizabethan manner." Believing drama to be one of the most effective modes of literary expression, both as a reflector and as a molder of society, Wendell maintains in his *Literary History* that vital theater in America was "rather sleeping than dead"; that, "if a dramatist of commanding power should arise in this country, he might find ready more than a few of the conditions from which lasting dramatic literature have flashed into being" (518). Consequently, Wendell "did not confine study of the drama to the explanation of ancient texts, but preached and taught the upbuilding of a worthy modern drama."[35] His interest in modern drama, belying the views that he detested or ignored contemporary literature, is seen both in the evidence of class lectures and his *Literary History* and in his participation in the Mermaid, a group of teachers, including Wendell, Santayana, Howe, Baker, and Carpenter, who met together primarily to discuss Ibsen, Strindberg, and the new European drama.

Testimony that Wendell's dramatic concerns fell on fertile soil can be found in the chapter entitled "Wendell Points the Way" in Wisner Kinne's biography of George Baker. By 1899, Baker had without much success published two books on speech and argumentation; and he had amassed a large background of knowledge on the theater. Wendell wrote at this point concerning these two areas:

"The time is coming, I think,—if indeed it be not come,—when for your own sake you ought to stop on one or the other, and force recognition as the first American authority in that which you keep," and a month later Wendell "showed the path to success"; "You ought to give some Lowell Lectures . . . on the stage conditions of the Elizabethan stage. . . . I doubt whether you realize the thoroughness of your present equipment."[36]

Baker's career at Harvard and then Yale needs no additional documentation, and he acknowledges Wendell's encouragement in that career in the dedication to his *Development of Shakespeare as a Dramatist* (1907): "To Barrett Wendell in gratitude for many years of stimulating companionship and unremitting acts of friendliness." He wrote Wendell in 1917: "More and more I have come to see that my teaching at all and any success which has been mine as a teacher I owe to you. . . . For correction, stimulation, even inspiration in the past, and for thirty odd years, I thank you."[37] That this debt had important ramifications becomes clear when we read from a later, more famous statement by Eugene O'Neill:

> Only those of us who had the privilege of membership in the drama class of George Pierce Baker in the dark age when the American theatre was still, for playwrights, the closed shop . . . can know what a profound influence Professor Baker . . . exerted toward the encouragement and birth of modern American drama. . . .
>
> But the most vital thing for us, as possible future artists and creators, to learn at that time (Good God! For anyone to learn anywhere at any time!) was to believe in our work and keep on believing. And to hope. He helped us to hope—and for that we owe him all the finest we have in memory of gratitude and friendship.[38]

Just as Wendell inspired Baker, so Baker inspired several generations of budding playwrights like O'Neill; his famous Harvard 47 workshop became a seminal force in the new drama emerging so clearly by the end of the 1920s. And Wendell again was the alchemy preceding the chemistry.

VI *Toward Art*

Nor did Wendell's influence stop there. As the patron-advisor of the *Harvard Monthly*, his office became the editorial room of the journal and his enthusiastic support of the fledgling publication brought Wendell into contact with, and gave encouragement to, such editors and contributors as Baker, Santayana, Mark Howe, Robert Herrick, William Vaughan Moody, Robert Morss Lovett, and Frank Norris. Walter Eaton, once a drama critic for the *New York Tribune* and later a Princeton professor of playwriting, described the significance of his former teacher, both as advisor and teacher of creative writing: "What Wendell did for Harvard was actually to make a place there . . . in which the artist could find encouragement and council."[39] Wendell knew that school tended to smother genius, but he felt that good education should instead stimulate it; consequently, he always attended to individual students. While his reputation marked him, as Paul More has said, as a "snob of the first water," students were struck by his personal warmth: "Meritorious effort and achievement and personal qualities were all that counted in his estimate of a man, however much he might theorize on the essential of background, birth, and breeding. He denied democracy, yet he gave the warmest consideration and the most special help to the boy who was poor, obscure, and self-supporting."[40]

A good example of such aid is the story told by W. E. B. DuBois, one of the most prominent black leaders and writers in the twentieth century, who at Harvard "was desperately afraid of not being wanted." The encouragement of a favorable response from Wendell following one of the famous in-class theme readings was remembered gratefully by DuBois years later when writing his autobiography. More important, however, was the reason DuBois enrolled in Wendell's English 12. His personal feelings had obscured the argument in a paper written previously for another course; so, believing "perhaps foolishly, but sincerely, that I have something to say to the world . . . I have taken English 12 in order to say it well."[41]

Such a story recurs often, for Wendell was the focal point for the creative energy that was spreading among the Harvard student body. And for many reasons; he was a teacher who respected art and an artist himself, who never minded making an exhibition of himself for art. He knew moreover that real art grew not out of the classroom but from real life—that a man like Mark Twain learned more from experiences on the Mississippi frontier than from any Back Bay parlor. He could talk shop, which was the nature of English 12, but his own lack of experience in isolated Cambridge and his frustrated career as a novelist made him painfully aware of himself as an inadequate substitute for the real thing of life. When Edwin Arlington Robinson told him he had left Harvard after two years, Wendell replied, "You're damn lucky!"[42]

Nevertheless, Wendell served as a guide to many literary aspirants in the 1890s as the man around whom creative writing at Harvard centered. Robert Frost entered Harvard to study with William James and attempted to bypass freshman composition, "hoping that he was qualified to take Barrett Wendell's course in advanced composition." Frank Norris moved to Cambridge with his mother explicitly for the purpose of enrolling in "one of the courses in creative writing for which Harvard had become famous through the work of Barrett Wendell and his associates."[43] Though he missed Wendell, he delighted in the English 12 focus on individual thinking and originality; and he began under Lewis Gates a novel called *McTeague*. The career of Robert Herrick offers still another case illustrative of Wendell's influence. It was in Wendell's course that this minor realistic novelist and Chicago professor first thought of a career as a novelist. Like so many other Harvard students he responded enthusiastically to Wendell's emphasis on individual perception and creativity, and later could say of Wendell: "He has had a greater influence upon the craftsmanship of the writer than any other American man of letters." At Wendell's retirement, he wrote: "My personal debt to Mr. Wendell is of the largest. . . . He taught me my profession, teaching, and he also gave me my first and my greatest inspiration in my art. . . . I am sure that I should never have taken my art with so much dignity and assurance, never have given it such devotion as I have tried to, had I escaped his influence."[44]

But Wendell's influence extended beyond just students at a time when universities, according to historians, were supposed bastions of aristocratic and traditionalist persuasion, and their professors safely guarded from the marketplace by ivory towers. Literary scholarship poked around in Anglo-Saxon manuscripts and in the cantos of Dante and left the modern world to spin itself out without academic interference or guidance. H. L. Mencken complained, "The very prince of gentlemanly critics was he who ignored literature altogether, thus attaining the ultimate in detachment from ignoble realities." So, at least, the anti-Victorians would have us believe. Yet to name Barrett Wendell as codefendant to this charge, as "immured by his Harvard professorship" to the real world, is to indulge in rather facile generalization. Not only in the focus of his

courses on the immediacy of experience necessary to the understanding of literature and composition, not only in his encouragement of would-be writers, but in his active effort to secure publication for creativity, Wendell demonstrated throughout a thirty-
seven-year career a vital attention to the mercury of contemporary
culture. He could accept much of it with difficulty, but dismiss it he
could not.

And a young colleague and former student shared his views, for
George Santayana, like Wendell, was unhappy with President
Eliot's antihumanist, proscience view. Santayana says of Wendell: "I
think that silently we essentially understood each other. We were
on the same side of the barricade. . . . What we deprecated was only
that this spontaneous life of the people should be frustrated by the
machinery of popular government, and of incorporated private interests." Santayana, of course, was a far more intelligent
philosopher and critic than Wendell; but Santayana owed a debt to
Wendell for helping launch his writing career. Santayana's first
book, the *Sense of Beauty*, had been thrown together from his
"sham course" in aesthetics in order to ensure the renewal of his
Harvard contract; but, unable to find a publisher, he "had given up
all expectation of getting it published when Barrett Wendell, always
friendly to me and the humanities, sent me word that he thought
Scribner's would accept it."[45] Wendell similarly introduced William
Lyon Phelps to Scribner's, for he served as "Charles Scribner's main
standby in Cambridge"; his involvement in the publication marketplace played a significant role in the development of "one of the
most successful and long-lived educational departments in the general publishing business," since, through Wendell, Scribner's "got
to know the men of Harvard's great days: Nathaniel Shaler, George
Herbert Palmer, Ralph Barton Perry and Wendell's protégés in
other universities: William Vaughan Moody, Robert Morss Lovett,
James Weber Linn, Charles Foster Kent—and a line of college
books grew up beside the school texts."[46]

In 1896, Edwin Arlington Robinson's volume of verse entitled
The Torrent and the Night Before introduced, not very successfully,
a new poet to the American scene only to be attacked by the genteel
critics who held ideality and beauty to be the only subjects of poetry, Warner Berthoff muses over how hard it is now "after the experimental novelties and triumphs of another half-century, to imagine the indifference of the established critical taste around 1900 to

the kind of poetic language Edwin Arlington Robinson and Robert
Frost . . . had begun teaching themselves to write in."[47] Not the
whole establishment, however, because in 1896 Barrett Wendell
wrote to Robinson: "very rarely, I think, does one find such work as
yours—where every line that meets the eye proves itself at a glance
real literature."

A tone of pleased surprise underlies Robinson's note to Wendell
thanking him "most sincerely for your kind and unexpected praise of
my experimental poems."[48] It is perhaps surprising to realize that
Wendell's poetic taste here failed to correspond with that of genteel
critics condemned for missing Robinson's importance, especially the
Robinson of his "most experimental" second volume, *Captain
Craig*, for it was through the letters of John Gardiner and Barrett
Wendell that the book received prepublication attention. Both Harvard teachers urged Scribner's to publish it, even going so far as
agreeing to underwrite the book's expense. Not even Theodore
Roosevelt was able to move W. C. Brownell at Scribner's, but the
incident puts Wendell solidly behind one of the major poets of the
new century.

To assess Wendell's relationship to Amy Lowell, we need once
more to turn to Van Wyck Brooks, who wrote that, as "Robinson was
the precursor of all the new poets, so also Amy Lowell was their
militant leader." When we then discover the lengthy correspondence (1915–1919) between Wendell and Lowell, we have evidence
not known to Brooks which makes the implicit contradiction already
noted in Brooks's estimate of Wendell explicit: while Wendell
never "shared the springtime faith . . . , never experienced the
American present," while he "symbolized the end of an epoch,"
while he "cherished a world that was gone," Amy Lowell stood for
energy central to the new literature.

If Boston's "tone was elegiac," in Wendell, it was renascent in
Lowell; she "begged, borrowed, stole, invented culture with a high
hand and a high heart." She was "the prime minister of the republic
of poets." Recognizing the appearance of a first-rate literary product, "she put her shoulder to the wheel and pushed it to market."
Like Brooks, she had nothing but distaste and scorn for the ivory-
towered Victorian professors who missed the literary activity going
on below their windows. For Brooks, then, Wendell stood for all
that was bad and Lowell for all that was good in Boston culture.[49]

But Amy Lowell wrote to Wendell in 1915, enclosing a copy of *Six French Poets*, "You have taught me so much in your books and in conversation, ever since I was a child, that I insist upon being considered in some sort your pupil."[50] The correspondence between Wendell and Lowell is illuminating, for Amy professed a serious indebtedness to her lifelong friend. She wrote in 1918 in response to his criticism of her "excess of vivacity," "That criticism of yours was one of the best I ever had" (76), and in 1917 she sent Wendell her *Tendencies in Modern American Poetry* (1917) and wondered "if it is not too much trouble, I will be very glad to have you tell me what you think of it, as I value your opinion very much." Wendell's response is typical of the long, detailed criticism that passed between them; her "friendly conservative" found that "the question is whether you have done a Literati, more thoughtful than Poe's . . . , or have cast the first light on ways to be. . . . That you have done work one would be glad to have done oneself is sure" (72). Wendell's long letter and Amy's seven-page response dealt frankly with her sense of a "new movement," characterized by a "marked Americanism," about which Wendell was quietly doubtful and Lowell clearly enthusiastic.

When Wendell's eight-page letter, following his reading of *Can Grande's Castle* (1918), warned Lowell to beware of an overabundant and intrusive rhyme and suggested "the hexameter line—or perhaps better still the elegiac couplet as a basis for polyphonic prose" (79), her reply recalls for us Wendell's critical conservatism and his inability to freely accept the new verse; but he could nonetheless offer positive advice. She wrote in 1918, "from you only do I ever get criticisms which are helpful, and although I may not appear in my work to benefit as much by them as you could wish, I assure you that they make a deep impression on me, and I often think of them when I am writing" (80). In one of his last letters to her, Wendell said, "Naturally—by nature, I mean—I am insensitive to lyric impressions. For many years, though, I have so struggled against this infirmity that I feel able to understand what lyric impression means. And here, even more than ever, you seem to me admirable in your purpose through out" (84).

Lowell's response—"I realize the difficulty of this new work in view of the old canons" (85)—is less marked than our own realization of the difficulty Wendell experienced. It was not easy for him to speak so positively about the new poetry; by nature, his feeling was that of Sara Orne Jewett, "We had better build more fences than take away from our lives," but more often he seems to straddle such fences; he wanted them up for protection but something in him also wanted them down. Waldo Frank said that, with Amy Lowell, American culture finally brought down that wall whose defenses had been manned by the eastern universities: "Quite literally she has trained her guns against her brothers," against those "forces which spoke in the United States Senate through such men as Henry Cabot Lodge; they preach in the schools through W. C. Brownell, Barrett Wendell, William Lyon Phelps."[51]

The times were changing, and Wendell was repeatedly found guilty by association with the old order, against which his age, his training, and his personality would not let him freely rebel; but as a teacher he helped sow the seeds of that rebellion. If American youth was rejecting Whittier, Bryant, Longfellow, Holmes, part of the reason was Barrett Wendell, whose often outrageous opinions in class—partly serious, generally ironic—led students to think for themselves. Wendell felt the ideal professor of literature "should be, in a word, as nearly as possible such a man as Arnold, or Lowell, or Sainte-Beuve." While he never felt he had achieved that character and while he also felt himself "too nearly tired out, . . . to be of much use in the new dispensation," he accurately claimed that his "true function was to keep a thread of way open for it [while] still in the Cimmerian midnight of the old."[52]

Wendell's pride in American literature led him to teach it; his professional awareness led him to point out its weaknesses. Such pride, coupled with an awareness of past failure, might well lend itself to a concern to make American literature new, to reevaluate its past. That many of the major twentieth-century artists, historians, and critics came out of Wendell's Harvard is fact—Joel Spingarn, George Santayana, Van Wyck Brooks, Bernard DeVoto, V. L. Parrington, T. S. Eliot, E. E. Cummings, Edwin Arlington Robinson, Robert Frost, John Dos Passos, Eugene O'Neill; how much of the Harvard atmosphere engendered by Wendell was conducive to cultural revolution must remain speculative. Nonetheless the feeling arises from observing Wendell's theories, his classroom techniques, and the response of many students, both famous and unknown, that Wendell's influence was larger than is usually true of a college instructor. We may be guilty of the *post hoc* fallacy but Walter Rollo Brown describes rather accurately the weight of evidence here:

When some one sits down to explain why in the early years of the twentieth century the younger readers and writers of America began to concern themselves with something less hollow, less conventionally formed than much of the literature conveniently styled "New England," he cannot leave Briggs and Wendell out of consideration. They trained men to look at the world with their own eyes, and to write directly and honestly about what they saw, without regard to the traditional ways of looking at things. . . . Only the blind can say that this fact has had nothing to do with our attempt, more or less national, to develop a literary art directly from the soil.[53]

A serious blindness has existed in American literary histories about the significance of Barrett Wendell. His books have been read, albeit narrowly; but the Harvard teacher and light-giver has been forgotten.

CHAPTER 8

A Problem in Literary History

BEYOND the insights gained from our exploration of the life and career of Barrett Wendell, the investigation itself is significant simply because few writers have seriously considered this Harvard professor since his death in 1921. To attempt such a study as this one involves more than curiosity about the identity of Barrett Wendell: it presents us with a problem created by the evolution of American literature and criticism in the twentieth century—an evolution characterized by strong distaste for American letters in the late nineteenth century. When we attempt to locate Wendell within the critical activity of the last century, we immediately encounter a modern recollection of Wendell as the epitome of all that was wrong with Victorian American critics.

In his own day, his status seemed assured; the 1926 collection of essays by his former students proclaimed that "the name of Barrett Wendell belongs to the literary tradition of America and needs no memorials to insure its enduring place in that tradition."[1] But we need only compare that comment with the characteristically negative response to Wendell by major twentieth-century critics and literary historians to realize how wide the chasm is that separates us from the writers of the genteel era. For instance, Van Wyck Brooks, as manifesto-giver for the early twentieth-century rebellion against the nineteenth, diagnosed Wendell's problem as "grandfather on the brain," and he regarded Wendell as a man who "stood for the seekers of the lost trails . . . , for those who felt their world had gone awry and who tried to grope their way back to an earlier time when life had been vigorous and hopeful."[2] Willard Thorp dismissed Wendell as one of the "Defenders of Ideality," hardened by his Harvard professorship to the realities of changing America; "he saved himself from . . . melancholy over the state of national culture . . . by means of his New England lineage, his Tory prejudices and his wit."[3] And Alfred Kazin has said, "as if to mark off for all time the difference between the literature that was passing and the new literature of the twentieth century, the famous Harvard professor of literature, Barrett Wendell, published in 1900 the last testament of the old school, *A Literary History of America.*"[4]

Such unsympathetic attitudes as these make it difficult, then, even to raise anew any question about the identity and the significance of Barrett Wendell; for the answer—"the last of the Boston Brahmins"—has been simple and has been given often. Yet to characterize Wendell as the last Tory, as the epitome of late nineteenth-century conservatism, as a narrow-minded anglophile, and as a sterile academic critic is to demonstrate the same narrowness of critical response of which his detractors have accused him and to demonstrate the critical barriers the twentieth century has raised against a part of its own past. Robert Falk maintains that the "critics and historians during the 1920's and 1930's succeeded in establishing by the skillful use of language and metaphor a system of attitudes toward that 'Victorian' generation which has influenced much of our thinking about it ever since."[5] So Thomas Beer described Wendell as "rather an emblem than a man, a vibrant point of protest against the vulgarization of American life, a realist in politics, a refugee among the dead in letters."[6] When we ask what Wendell was, we still encounter the Barrett Wendell who represents the decay of New England, the Indian Summer, the Gilded Age, the transcendental twilight, the Age of Innocence.

I *Surprising Praise*

William Dean Howells damned Wendell's *Literary History* and yet called it an important book because it offered a real challenge for readers interested in its subject. Wendell's life is just such a challenge to one interested in late nineteenth-century ideas, and that challenge is heightened by some unlikely twentieth-century critics. H. L. Mencken, Van Wyck Brooks, and Stuart Sherman (in his later phase as renegade from the Neo-Humanist cause) compose part of the group that Robert Spiller dubs the "Literary Radicals" to whom men like Wendell were anathema. Brooks repeatedly attacked the Puritan strain that Wendell found central to the American tradition, and Mencken had generally unkind words about "the professors." To them the literary artist was stifled by the emasculating culture still maintained by the older men; and Stuart Sherman joined this liberal camp in the late 1920s.

None of these men would we expect to praise Wendell; yet all three of them do—Brooks by implication and Mencken and Sherman explicitly. Brooks felt Wendell summarized all that he detested in nineteenth-century Boston; but, when he called Wendell one of the "Epigoni," he employed a double-edged metaphor, since the defeated sons of the seven who went against Thebes returned thirty years later to victory.[7] As we have observed, Amy Lowell represented for Brooks that victory of the old tradition in the new literature; and, while Brooks saw Wendell as a weak heir to the royalty of the 1840s in America's Athens, he was unaware of the important association between Lowell and Wendell. There is clearly truth in Brooks's generally accepted view of Wendell as a narrow-minded Brahmin who looked back for solace to a Tory past, but this view has obscured the Wendell who said that "it is best never to let the past cloud the future"—the man who, lacking the strength himself to grapple with the evolving new world, could transmit to students a faith which between 1900 and 1920 would lead them to proclaim America's Coming of Age.

In 1926, H. L. Mencken asked the question we now ask, "What remains, then, of Barrett Wendell, A.B., Litt.D.?" He responded, "Wendell's actual books, I believe, are now all dead," but not his influence: "when, indeed, the role of American literati is drawn up at last, and the high deeds of each are set down, it will be found that Wendell, too, did something, and that what he did was of considerable importance."[8] To Mencken, Wendell was an important humanist, a critic of "human experience under the Republic," a teacher to whom literature meant the expression of vital experience which he conveyed to his students.

And Sherman's view, equally affirmative, held Wendell to be "a figure of almost tragic interest, with an appeal to readers who may never have heard of his classroom, with an appeal to . . . the sense for a high adventure in very difficult circumstances."[9] These perceptive critics could see, as few did, the man beneath the profusion of temperamental opinion and defensive improvisation. We have overlooked from men whose names we remember such positive criticism of a man now forgotten, but the fact that the very writers whom we expect to dismiss Wendell praise him suggests several things: the conditioning of our expectations by twentieth-century critical stances; the complexity of both Wendell and his time; and, most of all, an importance not generally accorded Wendell. Just such views as these greatly underscore the need to reappraise late nineteenth-century Boston and one of its central personalities. Henry F. May, using less pejorative language than Spiller, described Wendell and his fellows as "Custodians of Culture" who must be given at least "the credit due sincerity and public spirit. Perhaps, looking back from long after their downfall, one can grant that their function, whether or not they performed it adequately, was potentially an important one."[10]

Barrett Wendell performed an important function. There is some validity (though a case can be made on both sides) in James Russell Lowell's belief that "before we have an American Literature, we must have an American criticism." And for all important American criticism there has been a long foreground. The many young intellectuals calling for truly American literature before Emerson's American Scholar address provides a not unlikely parallel to the voices, strong, if not wholly sympathetic, that preceded Van Wyck Brooks's twentieth-century Emersonian plea in *America's Coming-of-Age* (1915). Howard Mumford Jones agrees that Wendell opened important trails even if he could not travel them; he cites Wendell as one of three scholars (with Moses Coit Tyler and Charles F. Richardson) "who, sharing the New England predilections and the racial prejudices of their period, nevertheless laid the foundation for the modern study of American letters."[11] It would be possible to make an argument for an indebtedness on Brooks's part to his old teacher, for Brooks's concern for a usable past and honest self-expression, as we have seen, are not absent in Wendell's concerns. While the New England influence was dying, it did not die. And that very culture which Wendell defended asked, according to Brooks, not whence but "Whither did the road lead now?" Brooks answered that question with a telling list: Irving Babbitt, E. A. Robinson, Eugene O'Neill, T. S. Eliot, E. E. Cummings, Robert Frost—all of whom indicate that "New England was to have another springtime," and all of whom experienced Wendell's Harvard.[12] But Wendell's tradition, that of James Russell Lowell and Charles Eliot Norton, leads less to Brooks's manifesto, as he himself notes, than to that of T. S. Eliot's "Tradition and the Individual Talent."

II   *Cultural Transition*

T. S. Eliot maintains that the task of criticism is to preserve tradition "where a good tradition exists"; and, to the young progres-

sive writers before the war, the defenders of ideality, or the custodians of culture, were shoring up the wrong traditions: "ignoring"
Melville; "underrating" Poe; and "oversimplifying" Hawthorne,
Emerson, Whitman, and Twain, "they deprived the young artist of
the richest part of his national heritage."[13] The young writers like
Mencken, Brooks, Lowell, and Pound became cultural midwives as
they began defining or recovering the roots of a native literature and
making them available for new creative expression. This cultural
rebirth marked the end of the literature of the new provincial nation
and the beginning of the literature of the whole nation. The first
American "renaissance" of the 1850s was fading; the second "renaissance" of the 1920s was appearing.

In 1880, Richard Henry Stoddard described Pfaff's in New York as
a "centre of literary and artistic Bohemianism; I never went inside
the place. Once I walked down the steps and stood at the door. I saw
Walt Whitman and others inside, but through diffidence or some
other feeling I did not enter."[14] The story makes a nice tableau
depicting the relationship between the critics of the older school
and the writers who were forging a new literature. There is something sad, however, in the portrait of a man who recognizes the new
and his own distance from it, and something sad also emerges from
Barrett Wendell's feeling in 1896: "Personally, I have never felt in
my life so deep a spiritual sense of the terrible loneliness of us who
would maintain ideas of what is good and noble." Men like Wendell
did see the new country arising and passing their generation by: "As
a race, if we may use the term, we [in New England] are of the past;
so much so I fear, that in another century we shall almost have faded
away."[15] What effective criticism flowed from the pens of such writers as Wendell came despite their negative self-criticism, and the
nature of any positive influence they exerted has been effectively
embalmed in subsequent exaggerations of their negative mood to
illustrate genteel insensitivity, so that Wendell became merely a
"provincial schoolmaster."

III   Reevaluation

We cannot gainsay or even overstate the importance of the efforts
of early twentieth-century criticism that denounced Wendell and
his contemporaries, that led the call for a new literature, a more
usable past, a new culture. These critics laid the ground work for a

new age in American criticism and literary history, the aims and standards of which are ours today. The positive significance of these decades in preparing the way for a period in American letters, surely to be remembered as a major age of analysis, effectively overshadows the conservative forces against which they struggled; but there is an irony here in the fact that three decades of writers in the early twentieth century struggled to get beyond the narrow vision of the nineteenth century in order to establish a sound critical method of induction and objectivity—only to reveal the same narrowness toward the genteel writers that the new method was meant to replace.

History of any sort generally reveals as much about the historian as it does about the time and people he describes, and the manifesto writers after 1910 and the new historians of the 1920s held a concept of the Genteel Era which was not false; rather, it was a myth—a literary paradigm not unlike Wendell's theory of national inexperience, or Henry Adams's attitude toward the Virgin and the Dynamo. Theirs was a creative construction of the past, an imaginative evocation of the past which often results from man's effort to explain his own existence, to exalt himself in an environment which seems to threaten that existence. The anxiety of literary radicals in the first decade of the twentieth century to defend their revolt and to comprehend the responsibilities of American culture led to their search for a usable past, that is, an extension of their own time and needs into the past, "as if somehow culture could push civilization back to where it had gone astray and start it off once more aright."[16]

Morton Zabel is right when he says that "no special insight into the nature and crises of our time is needed to see why this condition is inevitable, and why any retreat to sentimentality, self-assurance, or complacency has taken on the appearance of a danger or an abdication of responsibility."[17] Nor is it difficult from our perspective of two world wars, the Depression, the bomb, to view that nineteenth-century world as so much simpler than ours and to forget that they too faced frightening issues and traumatic decisions, for they experienced the Civil War, Darwinism, national expansion, labor strife, industrialization. It is easy for us to forget that, by the end of that century, a man like Barrett Wendell, hedged on one side by a decadent Brahmin tradition and on the other by a potentially chaotic future could, no less than T. S. Eliot, easily agree with John Donne " 'Tis all in pieces, all coherence gone" or with Yeats that

"Things fall apart; the centre cannot hold;/Mere anarchy is loosed upon the world."

Alfred North Whitehead speaks of a "time-provinciality" which asserts modernity as a virtue in itself; and, as early as 1928, Norman Foerster warned against this very error in new attempts at reinterpretation: "the new estimates tend to be capricious, indicative of a provincialism of time (the measurement of past literature by the ideas and moods of a narrow present) far more insidious than that provincialism of place from which American criticism suffered in the last century."[18] Inevitably, the past must be reacted against, objected to, found fault with; but we cannot as many young critics of the early twentieth century attempted, simply repudiate or dismiss it. It is one thing to recognize the rather fully explored weaknesses of the Genteel Era, to recognize the inevitable confusion among younger innovators as they necessarily rebelled against the old order, to appreciate the value of such rebellion for later twentieth-century literary creativity, criticism, and history—but it is something else again to recognize that the almost mechanical dismissal of the last half of the nineteenth century has thrown a blanket of obscurity over the merits of that period. It is requisite to see the late nineteenth century, in Teddy Roosevelt's words, as "a certain grayness in the afternoon" and not in the usual blacks and whites, and to attempt a more objective, less defensive analysis of that complex and undervalued era.

In our attempt to identify Barrett Wendell we have found a figure of ambivalence, of contradictions, of surprises, of importance in the history of American letters. His infamous negativity about the quality of American literature was more than balanced by his belief that national American expression, American "inexperience," in 1900 was approaching the achievement of experience; and his *Literary History* helped bring about a reconsideration of American literary tradition and sparked new interest in the study of American literature.

His *English Composition*, far from reiterating traditional principles of rhetoric, initiated modern methods of teaching composition in the universities. With an intellectual appreciation of Puritan culture, he expressed not sterile Victorian prudishness but produced the best biography of Cotton Mather. His despair over the influx of . foreign immigrants and the threat to property implied by universal suffrage hardly outweighed his unflagging faith in democratic excellence. His prejudicial faith in the superior ability of the "better sort" did not deny excellence in minorities, nor did his supremely Tory sympathies prevent him from congenial encouragement of younger liberal intellectuals. Even his appreciation for the good and moral in literature failed to blind him to the more ultimate aesthetic qualities in Poe and Whitman.

Like his friend Henry Adams who felt himself to be living in a "weak transitional period," or like Eliot's Tiresias "throbbing between two lives," Barrett Wendell keenly felt the pressure of change but lacked the prophecy to assert its ultimate direction. We encounter repeatedly this stance in Wendell's writing: the future "shall prove most tremendously whether at this moment of crescent democratic force our world is passing into the dusk of a new barbarism, or into the dawn of a new dispensation." Wendell was not so appalled as Henry Adams by the vision of the future revealed at the 1893 Columbia Exposition in Chicago; he indecisively questioned, "is the white vanishing city a dawn-glow, shadowing in dreamy beauty the ideal splendor of the actual future? Is it more truly El Dorado, the last sunset glow of the fantastic aspiration of dying Europe?"[19] Wendell did not like Sandburg's Chicago, but with New England values almost extinct he saw the seeds of the future in the Midway. There were gray streaks in this new dawn sky, but he remembered that even in Dante's day the great splendors of Florence were yet to come. Theoretically, he could not denounce the changes he saw nor his own conservative role: "The great moments seem to me those when energy, which has been confined by tradition, breaks the outworn bonds of it. This was the case in New England, when New England was memorable. Nothing but conscious knowledge of orthodoxy could have made Emerson what he was."[20]

When Van Wyck Brooks said that "the real New England was not to be found in the Barrett Wendells," he might have easily said that this New England was nowhere to be found in all of Boston. While progressives are certainly as guilty of slighting the aristocratic class consciousness of New England as they are of ignoring the lower-class strata of nineteenth-century America, there is enough evidence of cultural vitality in Boston during the 1890s to refute Brooks's claim "that the steady decline upon which Boston entered following the Civil War touched bottom in the last years of the nineteenth century."[21] Part of this evidence lies in the golden years of Charles Eliot's Harvard wherein the appeal of men like Lowell,

Norton, and Wendell to the tradition of the Middle Ages, of Dante, of the late Elizabethans, of Donne, of Anglo-Catholic feeling, of Tory sentiments may mark the decline of a tradition but, as the early decades of this century reveal, not the end of it.

The South and New England after the Civil War had much in common with regard to the dissolution of an older society. Editors like Richard Watson Gilder appreciated the nostalgic reminiscence of antebellum days in southern fiction with something like the same impulse that Barrett Wendell recalled the Puritan days of Cotton Mather. Just as the South was to forge the traditions of an old heritage into new literature in the twentieth century, so too was New England to be part of a new century renaissance. Wendell gives us in his life and his works an adequate description of the Boston and Harvard attitudes between James Russell Lowell and T. S. Eliot. Asking where such a period belongs in human history, Wendell wrote, "surely not among the things that are great, but just as surely among the things that are significant. It is the moments of inspiration in human history that are great, but not less significant than the great moments are the periods of preparation."[22] Wendell's was such an interim period, when, its outward forms weakened, the spirit of the tradition of Norton and Lowell still lived, and Wendell paradoxically marks both its end and its continuance.

When William James wrote to Wendell in 1905 about being Wendell's successor in the Hyde lectures at the Sorbonne, he exclaimed, "You the Baptist! I the Messiah!!"[23] The image, in relation to Wendell, is not wholly facetious; for Wendell, who as a teacher hoped "we shall contribute our own part, great or small, to the already extensive American literature," was indeed a pioneer— in the teaching of creative writing, in the development of college composition courses, in the study of American literature, in the development of American studies programs. Wendell was a voice preparing the way, even though many who heard that voice denied its value in the 1920s and 1930s. Wendell once remarked about his role in the teaching of composition, "it took alchemy to make chemistry." While this phrase may perhaps describe the late nineteenth century in general, the "alchemy" in Wendell's laboratory at Harvard clearly led to much of the "chemistry" central to twentieth-century American literature.

Notes and References

Preface

1. George Santayana, "The Genteel Tradition in American Philosophy," in *Santayana on America, Essays, Notes, and Letters on American Life, Literature, and Philosophy*, ed. and intro., Richard Cotton Lyon (New York, 1968), p. 37.

Chapter One

1. "Recollections of My Father," Houghton Library, Harvard University, p. 49 (hereafter page numbers follow quoted material). This long family history was written for Wendell's children.

2. Wendell to his father, November 10, 1892, in Mark A. DeWolfe Howe, *Barrett Wendell and His Letters* (Boston, 1924), p. 106 (hereafter cited as *Letters*).

3. February 25, 1912, *ibid.*, p. 242. Wendell's praise of Roosevelt is in "Le President Roosevelt," *Revue Politique et Parlementaire*, February 10, 1905, pp. 7–15.

4. Walter P. Eaton, "Barrett Wendell," *American Mercury* 5 (August, 1925), 448–49.

5. Stuart P. Sherman, "Barrett Wendell: Farewell, New England Gentleman," in *Critical Woodcuts* (New York, 1926), p. 252.

6. H. L. Mencken, "The Last New Englander," in *Prejudices, Fifth Series* (New York, 1926), p. 250.

7. Wendell to Frederic Stimson, December 18, 1904, Howe, *Letters*, p. 162.

8. Wendell to Robert Thomson, December 17, 1893, Howe, *Letters*, p. 109.

9. Wendell to Robert Herrick, January 27, 1894, Howe, *Letters*, p. 109.

10. Sherman, p. 248.

11. George Santayana to William Lyon Phelps, *The Letters of George Santayana*, ed. Daniel Cory (New York, 1955), p. 332; Martin Green, *The Problem of Boston* (New York, 1966), p. 120.

12. Robert Herrick, "Barrett Wendell," *New Republic*, December 10, 1924, pp. 6–7.

13. Abbott Lawrence Lowell, "Memoir of Barrett Wendell," *Proceedings of the Massachusetts Historical Society* 55 (December, 1921), 184.

14. Henry James, *Charles W. Eliot*, 2 vols. (Boston, 1930), II, 134–35.

15. *A Literary History of America* (New York, 1900), p. 333.

16. Howe, p. 31.

17. Wendell to Robert Thomson, December 29, 1886, Howe, *Letters*, p. 68.

18. Sherman, p. 252.

19. "Selections from the Recent Correspondence of Hollis Alworthy," *Harvard Lampoon* 3 (June, 1877), 109–12.

20. Santayana, pp. 332–33.

21. Sherman, p. 253.

22. Wendell to Stimson, August 15, 1880, Howe, *Letters*, p. 47; and Wendell to Stedman, November 20, 1885 and January 7, 1892, Butler Library, Columbia University, New York.

23. Thomas Beer, *The Mauve Decade* (New York, 1926), pp. 82, 184.

24. Wendell to Mary Wendell, June 14, 1917, Howe, *Letters*, p. 278.

25. Honorary Degrees, Commencement, 1913, *Columbia University Quarterly* 15 (September, 1913), 342; Fernand Baldensperger, "Barrett Wendell: American 'Discoverer' of France," *The Living Age*, April 30, 1921, p. 284.

26. Roger Burlingame, "A Harvard Tradition," *Saturday Review of Literature*, October 18, 1924, p. 199.

27. George Santayana, *Persons and Places*, 3 vols. (New York, 1945), II, 171.

28. Edith Wendell Osborne, "Recollections of My Father, August 23, 1855–February 8, 1921" (Privately printed as a Christmas gift, 1921), pp. 12–15.

29. Wendell to Kittredge, October 15, 1890, Houghton Library, Harvard University; and Wendell to Mary Wendell, May 14, 1915, Howe, *Letters*, p. 268.

30. Wendell's three essays on Lowell appear in *Stelligeri* (New York, 1893), pp. 205–17; *A Literary History of America*, pp. 393–406; and *Commemoration of the Centenary of James Russell Lowell* (New York, 1919), pp. 40–51.

31. Mark A. DeWolfe Howe, *A Venture in Remembrance* (Boston, 1941), p. 152.

32. Mencken, p. 249.

33. Santayana, *Letters*, p. 333.

34. Wendell to Lodge, September 23, 1919, Howe, *Letters*, p. 316; and Wendell to James, September 22, 1902, in Mark A. DeWolfe Howe, ed., "A Packet of Wendell-James Letters," *Scribner's Magazine* 84 (December, 1928), 682 (hereafter cited as "Wendell-James Letters").

35. Beer, p. 183.

36. In *Henry Adams and His Friends*, ed. Harold Dean Cater (Boston, 1947), p. 644.

37. Fred Lewis Pattee, "A Call for a Literary Historian," in *The Reinterpretation of American Literature*, ed. Norman Foerster (New York, 1928), p. 22.

38. Santayana, *Persons and Places*, p. 171.

39. Wendell to White-Thomson, November 22, 1908, Howe, *Letters*, p. 198.

Chapter Two

1. Wendell to James, October 25, 1900, Howe, "Wendell-James Letters," pp. 677–78.

2. Alan Heimert, Introduction to Barrett Wendell, *Cotton Mather* (New York, 1963), p. xxii.

3. *Cotton Mather* (New York, 1891), p. 3 (hereafter page numbers follow quoted material).

4. Kenneth B. Murdock, "*Cotton Mather, the Puritan Priest*, by Barrett Wendell, '77," *Harvard Graduates' Magazine* 34 (June, 1926), 622–63; and Heimert, p. vii.

5. Mencken, p. 245; V. L. Parrington, *Main Currents in American Thought*, 3 vols. (New York, 1930), I, vi, 116.

6. "Wendell's 'Cotton Mather,' " *The Critic*, January 2, 1892, p. 1.

7. Lindsay Swift, "Cotton Mather," *The Nation*, December 1, 1892, p. 414.

8. "The American Intellect," in *The Cambridge Modern History*, 13 vols., ed. A. W. Ward *et al.* (New York, 1903), VII, 726.

9. Wendell to James, January 30, 1901, Howe, "Wendell-James Letters," pp. 678–81.

10. *Stelligeri*, p. 50.

11. *Ibid.*, p. 62.

12. Anon., "Briefs on New Books," *The Dial* 12 (March, 1892), 393.

13. Heimert, p. xix.

14. "Francis Parkman," *Proceedings of the American Academy of Arts and Sciences* 29 (May 9, 1894), 446.

Chapter Three

1. Anon., "Professor Wendell's Optimism," *Putnam's Monthly* 1 (February, 1907), 639.

2. William MacDonald, review of *Liberty, Union, and Democracy*, *The Nation*, November 22, 1906, p. 444.

3. Letter to Robert Thomson, August 5, 1895, Howe, *Letters*, pp. 112–13.

4. "The Ideals of Empire," *Harvard Graduates' Magazine* 25 (June, 1917), 474.

5. *Liberty, Union, and Democracy* (New York, 1906), p. 2 (hereafter page numbers follow quoted material).

6. Van Wyck Brooks, *New England: Indian Summer, 1865–1916* (New York, 1940), p. 426; and *An Autobiography* (New York, 1965), p. 110.

7. *The Privileged Classes* (New York, 1908), p. 63 (hereafter page numbers follow quoted material).

8. William MacDonald, "Wendell's Privileged Classes," *The Nation*, January 21, 1909, p. 69.

9. Horace Traubel, "Liberty Union and Democracy," *The Conservator* 17 (November, 1906), 141.

10. *The France of Today* (New York, 1907), p. 370 (hereafter page numbers follow quoted material).

11. Robert P. Falk, "The Literary Criticism of the Genteel Decades, 1870–1900," in *The Development of American Literary Criticism*, ed. Floyd Stovall (Chapel Hill, 1955), pp. 153–54.

12. J. J. Jusserand, "Barrett Wendell's France," *New York Times*, November 23, 1907, p. 742.

13. Lowell, p. 182.

14. Printed in Mark A. DeWolfe Howe, *La Vie et la Correspondance de Barrett Wendell*, tr. A. Brulé (Paris, 1926), p. 13.

15. James to Wendell, November 8, 1907, Howe, "Wendell-James Letters," p. 685.

16. Baldensperger, p. 281.

17. Traubel, p. 141.

18. So called by Clinton Rossiter, *Conservatism in America* (New York, 1955), p. 169.

Chapter Four

1. Wendell to E. K. Rand, April 19, 1920, Howe, *Letters*, p. 327.

2. William R. Castle, Jr., "Barrett Wendell, Some Memories of a Former Student," *Scribner's Magazine* 70 (July, 1921), 66.

3. Ferris Greenslet, "Wendell's Seventeenth-Century Literature," *The Nation*, December 29, 1904, p. 527.

4. *The Traditions of European Literature* (New York, 1920), pp. 1, 3 (hereafter page numbers follow quoted material).

5. Review of Edward Eggleston's *The Transit of Civilization*, *American Historical Review* 6 (July, 1901), 803–4.

6. Harry Hayden Clark, "Why Is Literary Criticism in America Worth Studying," in *The Achievement of American Criticism*, ed. Clarence Arthur Brown (New York, 1954), p. xiv.

7. René Wellek and Austin Warren, *Theory of Literature* (New York, 1956), p. 265.

8. René Wellek, *Concepts of Criticism* (New Haven, 1963), p. 43.

9. *William Shakspere* (New York, 1894), pp. 1–6 (hereafter page numbers follow quoted material).

10. Lecture TS, October 2, 1889, "Lecture Notes for English 17, 1889–1890," Harvard University Archives.

11. *The Temper of the Seventeenth Century in England* (New York, 1904), p. 209 (hereafter page numbers follow quoted material).

12. Donald Pizer, *Realism and Naturalism in Nineteenth Century American Literature* (Carbondale, Ill., 1966), p. 78.

13. While Wendell does not cite them explicitly in his texts, the bibliographies in *Shakspere, A Literary History of America,* and *Traditions of European Literature* reveal specific awareness of major evolutionary theorists and critics: J. A. Symonds, *Studies of the Greek Poets;* Ferdinand Brunetière, *Manual of the History of French Literature;* T. S. Perry, *English Literature of the Eighteenth Century;* John Fiske, *The History of New England;* W. E. H. Lecky, *A History of England in the Eighteenth Century.*

14. Edward E. Hale, Jr., "A New Book on Shakespeare," *The Dial* 18 (January, 1895), 13.

15. Wellek, *Theory,* p. 256.

16. "The Growth of Shakspere," TS, Harvard University Archives, p. 4.

17. Burlingame, "A Harvard Tradition," p. 199.

18. "Lecture Notes for English 14, 1887–1888," Harvard University Archives.

19. Castle, pp. 64, 62.

20. *English Composition* (New York, 1891), pp. 282 ff.

21. *Mystery of Education* (New York, 1909), p. 189.

22. Wellek, *Theory,* p. 17.

23. Wendell to James, November 19, 1907, Howe, "Wendell-James Letters," p. 686.

24. Brooks, *New England: Indian Summer,* p. 437.

25. Brooks, *Autobiography,* pp. 112–13.

26. Warner Berthoff, *The Ferment of Realism* (New York, 1965), p. 10.

27. Herbert Howarth, *Notes on Some Figures behind T. S. Eliot* (Boston, 1964), p. 89.

28. *The Mystery of Education,* pp. 115, 75–76.

29. T. S. Eliot, *The Sacred Wood* (New York, 1960), pp. xv–xvi.

30. Howarth, pp. 75, 127, 91.

31. Wendell to Edith Wendell, July 18, 1886, Howe, *Letters,* p. 64.

32. Larzer Ziff, *The American 1890's* (New York, 1966), p. 347.

33. "Lecture Notes for English 17."

Chapter Five

1. Perry Miller, Foreword to Moses Coit Tyler, *A History of American Literature: 1607–1765* (New York, 1962), p. 5.

2. Van Wyck Brooks, *The Confident Years, 1885–1915* (New York, 1952), p. 495; William P. Trent *et al., The Cambridge History of American Literature,* 4 vols. (New York, 1917), I, 14; and Willard Thorp, "Defenders of Ideality," in *Literary History of the United States,* ed. Robert E. Spiller *et al.,* 3d ed. (New York, 1963), p. 820.

3. William Dean Howells, "Professor Barrett Wendell's Notions of American Literature," *North American Review* 172 (April, 1901), 623–24.

4. T. S. Eliot, "American Critics," *Times Literary Supplement,* January 10, 1929, p. 24.

5. In Frederic Spiers, ed., *Studies in American Literature* (Philadelphia, 1901), pp. 87–88.

6. Eliot, "American Critics," p. 24.

7. *Stelligeri,* pp. 53–54 (hereafter page numbers follow quoted material).

8. T. S. Eliot, "American Literature," *The Atheneum,* April 25, 1919, p. 236.

9. 1904 "Collection of Lectures on American Literature," TS, Harvard University Archives.

10. "The American Intellect," p. 728.

11. Lewis E. Gates, "Professor Wendell's 'Literary History of America,' " *The Critic* 38 (April, 1901), 341.

12. Apparently the term "New England Renaissance" is Wendell's own coinage. Thomas Wentworth Higginson, Henry Boynton, Fred Lewis Pattee, and Stuart Sherman all attribute the term specifically to Wendell.

13. Brooks, *New England: Indian Summer,* p. 428.

Chapter Six

1. *A Literary History of America,* p. 207 (hereafter page numbers follow quoted material).

2. *Stelligeri,* p. 94.

3. *The Mystery of Education,* p. 236. It is interesting that T. S. Eliot also singles out Poe, Hawthorne, and Whitman for qualified praise similar to Wendell's: Poe's was a "peculiar originality"; in Poe, Hawthorne, Whitman "originality, if not the full mental capacity of these men, was brought out, voiced out, by the starved environment"—Eliot, "American Literature," pp. 236–37.

4. Eliot, "American Literature," p. 237.

5. Jay B. Hubbell, *The South in American Literature* (Durham, N.C., 1954), pp. 548–49.

6. "Edgar Allan Poe," in *Mystery of Education,* p. 202.

7. George J. Smith, "A Harvard View of Whitman," *The Conservator* 13 (August, 1902), 85–87, and 13 (September, 1902), 102–4. See also Horace Traubel, "Barrett Wendell Versus," *The Conservator* 15 (November, 1904), 141.

8. Smith, p. 103

9. 1904 "Collection of Lectures on American Literature," TS, Harvard University Archives.

10. *A History of Literature in America* (New York, 1904); hereafter page numbers follow quoted material. Wendell "submitted the *Literary History*, chapter by chapter, to an advanced class of students at Harvard College," which procedure "strengthened our conviction that the earlier book was historically sound"; he expresses his debt to the "critical collaboration" of his graduate students (v.).

11. Quoted in Arthur Hazard Dakin, *Paul Elmer More* (Princeton, 1960), pp. 85–86.

12. Pattee, p. 9.

13. Miller, pp. 8–9.

14. Eaton, p. 455.

15. Howard Mumford Jones, *The Theory of American Literature* (Ithaca, N.Y., 1965), p. 175.

16. Foerster, p. xii.

17. Harry Hayden Clark, "American Literary History and American History," in Foerster, pp. 186–89.

Chapter Seven

1. Henry F. May, *The End of American Innocence* (Chicago, 1959). p. 56.

2. William R. Castle, Jr., "Barrett Wendell—Teacher," in *Essays in Memory of Barrett Wendell*, eds. William R. Castle, Jr., and Paul Kaufman (Cambridge, Mass., 1926), p. 10.

3. Mencken, p. 254.

4. Samuel Eliot Morison, *The Development of Harvard University Since the Inauguration of President Eliot, 1869–1929* (Cambridge, Mass., 1930), p. 76.

5. *Ibid.*

6. *The Privileged Classes*, pp. 236–37.

7. *English Composition* (hereafter page numbers follow quoted material).

8. Adams Sherman Hill, *Principles of Rhetoric and Their Application* (New York, 1876), p. 5 (hereafter page numbers follow quoted material).

9. Wendell to Herrick, October 14, 1889, Howe, *Letters*, p. 100.

10. Eaton, p. 450.

11. George P. Baker, "Barrett Wendell (1855–1921)," *Harvard Graduates' Magazine* 29 (June, 1921), 571.

12. Lucia B. Mirrielees, *Teaching Composition and Literature in Junior and Senior High School* (New York, 1937), p. 197.

13. Santayana, *Persons and Places*, II, 172.

14. Herrick, p. 7.

15. John Hite, "Report to the American Literature Group of the Modern Language Association on the Teaching of American Literature," mimeographed (December, 1946), p. 2.

16. Chester N. Greenough, "Tribute to Barrett Wendell," *Proceedings of the Massachusetts Historical Society* 54 (February, 1921), 200.

17. Charles A. Wagner, *Harvard, Four Centuries and Freedoms* (New York, 1950), pp. 279–80.

18. Heimert, p. xxxix.

19. Herrick, p. 7.

20. Baker, p. 574.

21. Castle, *Essays*, p. 9.

22. 1886 letter to Norton, Norton Papers, Houghton Library, Harvard University.

23. Eaton, p. 451.

24. Baker, p. 572.

25. Eaton, p. 450.

26. Introduction to John A. Lomax, ed., *Cowboy Songs and Other Frontier Ballads* (New York, 1910), pp. iii–xv.

27. From a letter in the collection of tributes to Wendell on his retirement June 15, 1917, collected by George P. Baker, Houghton Library, Harvard University.

28. John M. Manly, *Specimens of the Pre-Shakesperian Drama* (New York, 1897), p. xiii.

29. From letters by Young, Tassin, and Thorndike in Baker's collection of tributes.

30. Kenneth Murdock, ed., *Selections from Cotton Mather* (New York, 1926), p. ix.

31. Arthur T. Quiller-Couch, *Shakespeare's Workmanship* (Cambridge, England, 1918), p. v. Wendell expressed surprise and delight at praise from both Quiller-Couch and Mrs. Edith Wharton, Howe, *Letters*, p. 326.

32. E. K. Rand, "Barrett Wendell, MAGISTRVM SALUTAT. DISCI-PVLVS EDVARDVS," *Harvard Graduates' Magazine* 26 (September, 1917), 174.

33. Horace M. Kallen, "Journey to Another World," in *College in a Yard*, ed. Brooks Atkinson (Cambridge, Mass., 1957), pp. 118–19. Kallen wrote to the author of the present study about his former teacher and friend: "To know of it fills me with a kind of religious satisfaction."

34. Horace M. Kallen, *Individualism—An American Way of Life* (New York, 1933), p. x; Sidney Ratner, ed. and intro., *Visions and Action, Essays in Honor of Horace M. Kallen* (New Brunswick, N.J., 1953), p. vi.

35. Castle, "Some Memories," pp. 63, 64.

36. Wisner Payne Kinne, *George Pierce Baker and the American Theatre* (Cambridge, Mass., 1954), p. 45. Kinne also attributes much of the undergraduate excitement over Ibsen, Tolstoy, Turgenev, Flaubert, Zola, Maupassant to Wendell (p. 35).

37. In Baker's collection of tributes to Wendell.

38. Eugene O'Neill, "Professor G. P. Baker," *New York Times*, January 13, 1935, IX, i.

39. Eaton, p. 450.

40. Mark A. DeWolfe Howe, "From a Graduate's Window: A Personality," *Harvard Graduates' Magazine* 26 (June, 1921), 585.

41. W. E. B. DuBois, *Dusk of Dawn, An Essay toward an Autobiography of a Race Concept* (New York, 1940), pp. 35–36.

42. Hermann Hagedorn, *Edwin Arlington Robinson* (New York, 1938), p. 138.

43. Lawrence Thompson, *Robert Frost, The Early Years, 1874–1915* (New York, 1966), p. 234; Franklin Walker, *Frank Norris, a Biography* (New York, 1932), p. 90.

44. Herrick, p. 7; and Baker's collection of tributes.

45. Santayana, *Persons and Places*, p. 157.

46. Roger Burlingame, *Of Making Many Books* (New York, 1946), pp. 152–54.

47. Berthoff, pp. 263–64.

48. Wendell's note is quoted in Hoyt C. Franchere, *Edwin Arlington Robinson* (New York, 1968), p. 36. Robinson's note of December 11, 1896, is in the Houghton Library, Harvard University. Robinson called Wendell one of the "three good friends" he made at Harvard, along with John Gardiner and Daniel Gregory Mason.

49. Brooks, *New England: Indian Summer*, pp. 525, 426–27, 532–33.

50. Lowell to Wendell, November 21, 1915, in Robert T. Self, ed., "The Correspondence of Amy Lowell and Barrett Wendell, 1915–1919," *The New England Quarterly* 47 (March, 1974), 67 (hereafter page numbers follow quoted material).

51. Waldo Frank, *Our America* (New York, 1919), p. 163.

52. Wendell to Horace M. Kallen, October 15, 1911, Howe, *Letters*, p. 239.

53. Walter Rollo Brown, *Dean Briggs* (New York, 1926), p. 59.

Chapter Eight

1. Castle, *Essays*, p. 1.

2. Brooks, *New England: Indian Summer*, p. 425.

3. Thorp, "Defenders of Ideality," p. 820.

4. Alfred Kazin, *On Native Grounds* (New York, 1956), p. 42.

5. Robert P. Falk, *The Victorian Mode in American Fiction, 1865–1885* (East Lansing, Mich., 1965), p. 3.

6. Beer, pp. 183–84.

7. Brooks, *New England: Indian Summer*, p. 431.

8. Mencken, pp. 247–48.

9. Sherman, p. 249.

10. May, p. 31.

11. Jones, p. 99.

12. Brooks, *New England: Indian Summer*, p. 433.

13. Richard Ruland, *The Rediscovery of American Taste* (Cambridge, Mass., 1967), p. 114.

14. Richard Henry Stoddard, *Recollections Personal and Literary*, ed. Ripley Hitchcock (New York, 1903), p. 266.

15. Wendell to Charles Eliot Norton, Houghton Library, and to Charles H. Barrow, Jr. (1916), Harvard University Archives.

16. John H. Raleigh, "Revolt and Revolution in Criticism, 1920–1930," in Stovall, p. 162.

17. Morton D. Zabel, ed., *Literary Opinion in America*, 2 *vols.* (New York, 1956), I, xiv.

18. Foerster, p. xiii.

19. "Impressions at Chicago," TS, Houghton Library, Harvard University, p. 41.

20. Wendell to Frederick Schenck, August 28, 1906, Howe, *Letters*, p. 178.

21. Brooks, *New England: Indian Summer*, p. 473.

22. 1890 Lecture TS, Harvard University Archives.

23. James to Wendell, February 8, 1905, Howe, "Wendell-James Letters," p. 684.

Selected Bibliography

PRIMARY SOURCES

1. Books

The Duchess Emilia: A Romance. Boston: Osgood, 1885.

Rankell's Remains: An American Novel. Boston: Ticknor, 1887.

Cotton Mather, The Puritan Priest. Makers of America Series. New York: Dodd, Mead, 1891.

English Composition. New York: Scribner's, 1891.

Stelligeri, and Other Essays Concerning America. New York: Scribner's, 1893.

William Shakspere: A Study in Elizabethan Literature. New York: Scribner's, 1894.

A Literary History of America. The Library of Literary History. New York: Scribner's, 1900.

Ralegh in Guiana, Rosamond and a Christmas Masque. New York: Scribner's, 1902.

A History of Literature in America. In collaboration with Chester Noyes Greenough. New York: Scribner's, 1904.

The Temper of the Seventeenth Century in English Literature. New York: Scribner's, 1904.

Selections from the Writings of Joseph Addison. Ed., intro. and notes, in collaboration with Chester Noyes Greenough. Athenaeum Press Series. New York: Ginn, 1905.

Liberty, Union, and Democracy, the National Ideals of America. New York: Scribner's, 1906.

The France of Today. New York: Scribner's, 1907.

The Privileged Classes. New York: Scribner's, 1908.

The Mystery of Education, and Other Academic Performances. New York: Scribner's, 1909.

La France d'aujourd'hui. Tr. Georges Grappe. Paris: Floury, 1910.

The Traditions of European Literature from Homer to Dante. New York: Scribner's, 1920.

Einhard. *The History of the Translation of the Blessed Martyrs of Christ, Mercellinus and Peter.* Translated by Barrett Wendell. Cambridge: Harvard Univ. Press, 1926.

2. Articles

Editorial Contributions to *Harvard Lampoon*, vols. 1–7 (1876–1879).

"On Dinners and Dining." *Harvard Lampoon* 1 (June, 1876), 102–4.

"Notes on the Pedigree of Some of Our Contemporaries." *Harvard Lampoon* 3 (May, 1877), 689.

"Letters to a Freshman." *Harvard Advocate*, February 2, 1881, pp. 10–12.

"From a Looker-on in Chicago." *Boston Daily Advertiser*, July 10–11, 1884, pp. 1, 2.

"Social Life at Harvard." *Lippincott's Magazine* 39 (January, 1887), 152–63.

"The Last of the Ghosts." *Scribner's Magazine* 3 (February, 1888), 227–39.

"Mr. Lowell as a Teacher." *Scribner's Magazine* 10 (November, 1891), 645–49.

"Some Neglected Characteristics of the New England Puritans." *Annual Report of the American Historical Association for 1891.* Washington: American History Association, 1892.

"The Dean of Bourges." *Scribner's Magazine* 11 (January, 1892), 117–20.

"Were the Salem Witches Guiltless?" *Historical Collections of the Essex Institute*, 29 (February, 1892), 129–147.

"How He Went to the Devil." *Two Tales*, April 30, 1892, pp. 4–8.

"John Greenleaf Whittier." *Proceedings of the American Academy of Arts and Sciences* 27 (May, 1893), 431–41.

"Impressions at Chicago." *Harvard Monthly* 9 (October, 1893), 7–8.

"English Work in the Secondary Schools." *School Review* 1 (1893), 638.

"English at Harvard." *The Dial* 16 (March, 1894), 131–33.

"Francis Parkman." *Proceedings of the American Academy of Arts and Sciences* 29 (May, 1894), 435–47.

"Harvard University." *English in American Universities.* Ed. and intro. William Morton Payne. Boston: Heath, 1895.

Introduction. William Shakespeare, *As You Like It.* Longman's English Classics. New York: Longman, Green, 1896.

"Cotton Mather." *American Prose.* Ed. George Rice Carpenter. New York: Macmillan, 1898.

"Composition in the Elementary Schools." *New York Teachers' Monographs* 1 (November, 1898), 68–76.

"Samuel Eliot." *Proceedings of the American Academy of Arts and Sciences* 34 (May, 1899), 646–51.

"The Relations of Radcliffe College with Harvard." *Harvard Monthly* 14 (October, 1899), 3–11.

Introduction to John Hays Gardiner, *The Forms of Prose English.* New York: Scribner's, 1900.

"Memoir of William Whitwell Greenough." *Proceedings of the Massachusetts Historical Society* 34 (February, 1901), 1–17.

Review of *A Life of Francis Parkman* by Charles H. Farnham. *American Historical Review* 6 (January, 1901), 376–77.

Review of *The Clergy in American Life and Letters* by Daniel D. Addison. *American Historical Review* 6 (April, 1901), 576–79.

Review of *The Transit of Civilization from England to America in the Seventeenth Century* by Edward Eggleston. *American Historical Review* 6 (July, 1901), 802–5.

"A Review of American Literary Phases." *Studies in American Literature.* Ed. Frederic Spiers. Philadelphia: Booklovers' Library Press, 1901.

Review of *The Literary Diary of Ezra Stiles, D.D., LL.D., President of Yale College* by Franklin B. Dexter, ed. *American Historical Review* 7 (July, 1902), 769–72.

"The American Intellect." *The Cambridge Modern History*, vol. VII. Ed. A. W. Ward *et al.* New York: Cambridge Univ. Press, 1903.

"Our National Superstition." *North American Review* 179 (September, 1904), 388–401.

"Le President Roosevelt." *Revue Politique et Parlementaire*, February 10, 1905, pp. 7–15.

"Impressions of Contemporary France: The Universities." *Scribner's Magazine* 41 (March, 1907), 314–26.

"Impressions of Contemporary France: The Structure of Society." *Scribner's Magazine* 41 (April, 1907), 450–64.

"Impressions of Contemporary France: The French Temperament." *Scribner's Magazine* 41 (June, 1907), 741–53.

"Impressions of Contemporary France: The Republic and Democracy." *Scribner's Magazine* 42 (July, 1907), 53-65.

"The Influence of the Athenæum on Literature in America." *The Influence and History of the Boston Athenaeum from 1807 to 1907.* Ed. Albert Thorndyke. Boston: Boston Athenaeum, 1907.

"The Privileged Classes." *Journal of Education*, February 27, 1908, pp. 11–24.

"A Fantasy Concerning an Epitaph of Shakspere." *Anniversary Papers by Colleagues and Pupils of George Lyman Kittredge.* Boston: Ginn, 1908.

"The United States and France." *International Conciliation* 9 (August, 1908), 3–9.

"Charles Eliot Norton." *Atlantic Monthly* 103 (January, 1909), 82–88.

"Abbott Lawrence Lowell, Twenty-Fourth President of Harvard College." *Harvard Graduates' Magazine* 17 (March, 1909), 397–403.

"De Praeside Magnifico." *Harvard Graduates' Magazine* 18 (September, 1909), 26.

"Henry Cabot Lodge, Statesman." *Boston Herald*, May 1, 1910, p. 2.

Introduction. John A. Lomax, *Cowboy Songs and Other Frontier Ballads.* New York: Sturgis and Walton, 1910.

"Cotton Mather." *American Prose, Selections with Critical Introductions.* Ed. George Rice Carpenter. New York: Macmillan, 1911.

"Edmund March Wheelwright." *Harvard Graduates' Magazine* 21 (December, 1912), 240–42.

"A New England Puritan." *The Quarterly Review* 218 (January, 1913), 32–48.

Speech at the Alumni Luncheon. *Columbia University Quarterly* 15 (September, 1913), 355–56.

"The Mystery of Education." *Representative Phi Beta Kappa Orations.* Ed. Clark Sutherland Northrup. Boston: Houghton Mifflin, 1915.

"William Roscoe Thayer." *Harvard Graduates' Magazine* 24·(September, 1915), 19–22.

"Henry James: An Appreciation." *Boston Evening Transcript*, March 16, 1916, p. 20.

"The Ideals of Empire." *Harvard Graduates' Magazine* 25 (June, 1917), 458–74.

"Japan and Righteousness." *Scribner's Magazine* 64 (July, 1918), 71–79.

"Thomas Raynesford Lounsbury (1838–1915)." *Proceedings of the American Academy of Arts and Sciences* 53 (September, 1918), 831–40.

"The Conflict of Idolatries." *Harvard Graduates' Magazine* 27 (September, 1918), 1–16.

"Law and Legislation." *Scribner's Magazine* 65 (February, 1919), 177–81.

"A Gentlewoman of Boston, 1742–1805." *Proceedings of the American Antiquarian Society* 29 (October, 1919), 242–93.

"Sunrise." *Scribner's Magazine* 66 (October, 1919), 467–72.

"James Russell Lowell." *Commemoration of the Centenary of the Birth of James Russell Lowell.* New York: Scribner's, 1919.

SECONDARY SOURCES

ATKINSON, BROOKS, ed. *College in a Yard, Minutes by Thirty-Nine Harvard Men.* Cambridge: Harvard Univ. Press, 1957. Contains recollections of Wendell as a teacher by Horace Kallen and others.

BAKER, GEORGE PIERCE. "Barrett Wendell (1855–1921)." *Harvard Graduates' Magazine* 29 (June, 1921), 571–76. Personal recollections and appreciation for Wendell the teacher and the man.

BALDENSPERGER, FERNAND. "Barrett Wendell: American 'Discoverer' of France." *The Living Age*, April 30, 1921, pp. 280–84. Comments on Wendell's study of France and French appreciation of his work.

BEER, THOMAS. *The Mauve Decade.* New York: Knopf, 1926. Brief mention throughout of Wendell's personality.

BOLCE, HAROLD. "Polyglots in the Temples of Babel." *Cosmopolitan* 47 (June, 1909), 52–65. With something of a muck-raking concern, attempts to expose the "un-American" political attitudes of university men like Wendell.

BRIGGS, LEBARON R. "Enviable Record Here." *Harvard Crimson*, March 30, 1917, p. 5. Brief review of Wendell's career on his retirement.

BROOKS, VAN WYCK. *The Confident Years, 1885–1915.* New York: Dutton, 1952.

――――. *New England: Indian Summer, 1865–1916.* New York: Dutton, 1940. Both books contain passages citing Wendell as illustrative of Boston and Harvard attitudes distasteful to Brooks.

CASTLE, WILLIAM R., JR. "Barrett Wendell, Some Memories of a Former Student." *Scribner's Magazine* 70 (July, 1921), 60–66. Insights into Wendell's strengths as a teacher.

――――, and PAUL KAUFMAN, eds. *Essays in Memory of Barrett Wendell by His Assistants.* Cambridge: Harvard Univ. Press, 1926. First two essays recall Wendell as teacher and critic; the others are literary analysis.

DIMNET, M. ERNEST. "Results of a Literary Invasion." *Harper's Weekly*, July 29, 1905, p. 1092. Mixed reaction to Wendell's year at the Sorbonne.

EATON, WALTER P. "Barrett Wendell." *The American Mercury* 5 (August, 1925), 448–55. One of the most positive appraisals of Wendell's influence at Harvard.

ELIOT, T. S. "American Critics." *Times Literary Supplement*, January 10, 1929, p. 24.

――――. "American Literature." *The Atheneum*, April 25, 1919, pp. 236–37. Reviewing American literary history and criticism, Eliot finds strengths and weaknesses in Wendell.

FITZPATRICK, FRANK A. "Reflections of an Iconoclast." *Educational Review* 29 (February, 1905), 151–62. Attacks Wendell's views of public education as unscientific and reactionary.

GATES, LEWIS E. "Professor Wendell's 'Literary History of America.'" *The Critic*, April 4, 1901, pp. 341–44. Critical review by Wendell's colleague.

GRANT, ROBERT. "Tribute to Barrett Wendell." *Proceedings of the Massachusetts Historical Society* 54 (February, 1921), 198–99. Recollection from an old friend.

GREENOUGH, CHESTER NOYES. "Tribute to Barrett Wendell." *Proceedings of the Massachusetts Historical Society* 54 (February 1921), 199–202. Valuable insight about Wendell's role in the Harvard English Department by a former assistant and colleague.

HALL, FREDERICK G., EDWARD R. LITTLE, and HENRY WARE ELIOT, JR. *Harvard Celebrities, a Book of Caricatures and Decorative Drawings.* Cambridge: Harvard Lampoon, 1901. Contains a satirical poem and drawing of Wendell.

HERRICK, ROBERT. "Barrett Wendell." *The New Republic*, December 10, 1924, pp. 6–7. Strong praise for Wendell's influence at Harvard.

HOWARTH, HERBERT. *Notes on Some Figures behind T. S. Eliot.* Boston: Houghton, Mifflin, 1964. Contains Howarth's speculations as to Wendell's influence on Eliot.

HOWE, MARK A. DEWOLFE, ed. "A Packet of Wendell-James Letters." *Scribner's Magazine* 84 (December, 1928), 675–87. Correspondence between Wendell and his longtime friend William James.

————. *Barrett Wendell and His Letters.* Boston: Atlantic Monthly Press, 1924. Only other full length study of Wendell; nicely balanced comment about Wendell, his life, his personality, and his work; copiously illustrated by his letters.

————. "From a Graduate's Window: A Personality." *Harvard Graduates' Magazine* 29 (June, 1921), 583–86. Reminiscence at Wendell's death by the longtime friend.

HOWELLS, WILLIAM DEAN. "Professor Wendell's Notions of American Literature." *North American Review* 172 (April, 1901), 623–40. Howells's review both praises and damns Wendell's *History.*

JONES, HOWARD MUMFORD. *The Theory of American Literature.* Ithaca: Cornell Univ. Press, 1965. Several passages devoted to the significance of Wendell's *Literary History* in the development of American literary study.

JUSSERAND, JEAN JULES. "Barrett Wendell's France." *New York Times Saturday Review of Books,* November 23, 1907, p. 742. Praise of Wendell's book on France by the French ambassador to the United States.

KINNE, WISNER PAYNE. *George Pierce Baker and the American Theatre.* Cambridge: Harvard Univ. Press, 1954. A very good chapter describes Wendell's influence on Baker.

LEGOUIS, EMILE. "Barrett Wendell et la France." *Harvard et la France.* Paris: Revue d'histoire moderne, 1936. Assessment of Wendell's lectures at the Sorbonne and other French universities, and of his book *The France of Today.*

LEWIS, R.W.B. *Edith Wharton, a Biography.* New York: Harper and Row, 1975. Passages throughout the book describe the nature of Wendell's relationship with Wharton.

LODGE, HENRY CABOT. "Tribute to Barrett Wendell." *Proceedings of the Massachusetts Historical Society* 54 (February, 1921), 202–3. Rather stiff letter of praise sent to the Society from Washington.

LOWELL, ABBOTT LAWRENCE. "Memoir of Barrett Wendell." *Proceedings of the Massachusetts Historical Society* 55 (December, 1921), 174–85. Recollection by the Harvard president and old friend about Wendell's personality and relations with the university; incisive comments as to the complexity of Wendell's character.

MACY, JOHN. "Professor Wendell's 'The Privileged Classes.'" *The Bookman* 28 (December, 1908), 357–59. Analyzes conflicting perspectives in one of Wendell's most controversial works.

MATTHEWS, BRANDER. "Our Literary Heritage from Europe." *New York Times Book Review*, December 26, 1920, p. 3. Positive review of Wendell's *Traditions of European Literature*.

MAY, HENRY F. *The End of American Innocence, A Study of the First Years of Our Time*. Chicago: Quadrangle, 1959. Comments here and there on Wendell's role as one of the late nineteenth-century "custodians of culture."

MENCKEN, H. L. *Prejudices, Fifth Series*. New York: Knopf, 1926. Contains Mencken's highly positive evaluation of Wendell as teacher, humanist, eccentric.

MORISON, SAMUEL ELIOT, ed. *The Development of Harvard University Since the Inauguration of President Eliot, 1869–1929*. Cambridge: Harvard Univ. Press, 1930. Contains valuable facts about Wendell's career at Harvard.

NOXON, FRANK W. "College Professors Who Are Men of Letters." *The Critic* 42 (February, 1903), 124–35. Indicates something of the popular reputation Wendell enjoyed.

OSBORNE, EDITH WENDELL. *Recollections of My Father, August 23, 1855–February 8, 1921*. Privately published, 1921. Reminiscence about Wendell and Wendell family life by one of Wendell's daughters.

PLATT, ISAAC HULL. "Wendell on Whitman: Criticism or Libel." *The Conservator* 13 (October, 1902), 118–19. Harsh reaction against Wendell by the Whitman Fellowship.

POWELL, G. H. "The Mind of America." *Contemporary Review* 82 (July, 1902), 111–25. Lengthy discussion of values and weakness in Wendell's *Literary History*.

RHODES, JAMES FORD. "Tribute to Barrett Wendell." *Proceedings of the Massachusetts Historical Society* 54 (February, 1921), 195–98. Eulogistic description of Wendell's personality and career.

SAINTSBURY, GEORGE. "From Homer to Dante." *Bookman* (London) 61 (October, 1921), 19–20. Largely negative review of Wendell's *Traditions of European Literature*.

SANTAYANA, GEORGE. *The Letters of George Santayana*. Ed. Daniel Cory. New York: Scribner's, 1955.

———. *Persons and Places*. Vol. II: *The Middle Span*. New York: Scribner's, 1945. Santayana's recollections of Wendell's eccentric personality and his friendship at Harvard are scattered throughout both works.

SELF, ROBERT T., ed. "The Correspondence of Amy Lowell and Barrett Wendell, 1915–1919." *The New England Quarterly* 47 (March, 1974), 65–86. Valuable letters from the Amy Lowell Collection at Harvard offer insight into the relationship of two important New Englanders from different generations.

SHERMAN, STUART P. *Critical Woodcuts*. New York: Scribner's, 1926. Informative, positive insight into Wendell's contributions as a teacher by a member of Brooks's generation.

SMITH, GEORGE. "A Harvard View of Whitman," Pt. 1 *The Conservator* 13 (August, 1902), 85–87, and Pt. 2, 13 (September, 1902), 102–4. Another pro-Whitman reaction against Wendell's *Literary History*.

STIMPSON, MARY STOYELL. "The Harvard Lampoon: Its Founders and Famous Contributors." *New England Magazine* 35 (January, 1907), 579–90. Comments on Wendell's role in the early years of the *Lampoon*.

THWING, CHARLES FRANKLIN. *Friends of Men*. New York: Macmillan, 1933. Almost emotional chapter of recollections about Wendell as a teacher.

TRAUBEL, HORACE. "Barrett Wendell Versus." *The Conservator* 15 (November, 1904), 141.

———. "Liberty Union and Democracy." *The Conservator* 17 (November, 1906), 140–41. Harsh liberal attacks in both articles against Wendell's political and social views.

Index